Lead us to Purity

A collection of the teachings of
Sri Mata Amritanandamayi

Compiled by Swami Jnanamritananda

Mata Amritanandamayi Center
San Ramon, California, United States

Lead us to Purity

A collection of the teachings of Sri Mata Amritanandamayi
Compiled by Swami Jnanamritananda
English translation by M.N. Namboodiri

Published by:
Mata Amritanandamayi Center
P.O. Box 613
San Ramon, CA 94583-0613, USA

First edition MA Center: 2015

In India:
www.amritapuri.org
inform@amritapuri.org

In USA:
www.amma.org

In Europe:
www.amma-europe.org

O Supreme Being,
lead us from untruth to truth,
from darkness to light,
and from death to immortality.
Om peace, peace, peace.

– Brihadaranyaka Upanishad (1:3:28)

Contents

Foreword

This book contains a collection of speeches that Amma gave in India between 1990 and 1999. As Amma reveals the truths of life in the light of spirituality and in a manner unassailable by logic, the reader is given not only a fresh view of life, but is inspired to live according to the universal principles that Amma explains in such a crystal clear way. Like a mother talking to her child, Amma brings profound principles to light through the simplest of words. In this book we are given compelling answers to the numerous questions that most of us have asked or have wanted to ask at one time or another.

The reader will find that a few of the speeches contain the same examples or stories. These rare repetitions have been left as they are, because the examples are so beautiful and fit so marvelously into the context of the text, and because the editors didn't want to tamper with Amma's speeches in any way.

Every sentence uttered by Amma helps us to understand the ultimate aim of life, and reveals paths to the realization of that goal. Amma's words guide and encourage us towards a truly full and meaningful life.

Part one

Children of Immortality

Amma's birthday messages

May my verses go forth like the sun on its path.
May all the children of immortality listen,
even those who have ascended to heaven.

– Shvetashvatara Upanishad (2:5)

Amma after the pada puja at her birthday celebration

Practicing dharma is the source and sustenance of dharma

Amma's birthday message 1990

During Amma's birthday celebrations in 1990 about 20,000 people from all walks of life and from throughout India attended, and hundreds of people from the West participated as well. By the late nineties the crowds had swelled to more than 50,000.

My dear children, [1]

It pleases Amma [2] that on her birthday you are so happy and are doing selfless service.

Beyond this, Amma gets no special joy out of these celebrations. Amma has agreed to all of this only to see the happiness of her children. My dear children, it truly gladdens Amma to see you loving one another and being compassionate towards others. It also pleases Amma much more when you volunteer to clean a dirty sewer nearby than when you wash her feet and worship them. Be willing to serve the world with as much devotion and passion as you show in serving Amma. Real worship of Amma's feet is to selflessly strive to remove the suffering in the world. It would make Amma truly happy if her children were to consider her birthday as the day for wiping the tears of the suffering.

Cultivate an attitude of renunciation

If you love Amma and want her to be happy, take a vow to give up at least one bad habit on each of her birthdays. That

---

[1] Amma refers to people as her children or her sons and daughters. When she talks about people, she often says, "the children."

[2] Amma means 'Mother' in Malayalam. Amma usually refers to herself in the third person as 'Amma'.

would show your true love for Amma. If happiness really resided in cigarettes, for instance, wouldn't everyone be able to get happiness out of smoking? But that is not the case. Some people can't stand the smell of cigarettes; it makes them agitated. Happiness doesn't depend on objects; happiness depends on the mind. By bringing our minds under control, we can experience joy without the help of any external objects. So, why waste money and risk your health? Those of you who smoke, take a vow to quit smoking from this day on. The money you save in this way can be spent on the education of a destitute child. Those of you who drink alcohol, take a vow to stop drinking. Also, between one hundred and five hundred rupees are often spent on a single item of clothing. Some of you buy at least ten saris a year. Make that nine this year, and spend that extra money on medicine for a destitute person who is sick. If you children love Amma, if you love the Supreme Being, you should be willing to adopt such an attitude of renunciation.

My children, we cannot realize God without renunciation. *Tyagenaike amritatvamanashuh* – "Only through renunciation can one attain immortality." To attain any goal, we have to give up something. To pass an examination, we have to study hard, keeping that goal in mind. If we want to build a bridge, we have to work with a great deal of care and patience. The basis of success in any endeavor is the act of renunciation. We cannot cross the ocean of *samsara*[3] without the spirit of renunciation. Without renunciation, chanting mantras won't bring any benefit. Regardless of how many times we chant a mantra, we cannot realize our beloved deity[4] (*ishta devata*) without the spirit of renunciation. The deity will appear before one who has this spirit, even if he

---

[3] The world of plurality; the cycle of birth, death, and rebirth.

[4] The Divinity one has chosen to worship in accordance with one's own nature, and which is the object of one's greatest desire and ultimate goal.

or she doesn't repeat a mantra. All the divine beings will come to assist such a person in his or her work. This doesn't mean that we needn't chant a mantra, only that we also have to live up to those principles. Sowing a seed is not enough. Perfection is achieved when good deeds are performed with the attitude of renunciation. Our good actions show how much we have grown.

Compassion towards the poor is our duty to God

We worship in the temple by circumambulating the temple and calling out "Krishna! Krishna!" and then, as we leave the place, the beggars at the door may be pleading, "Help me! I'm starving!" But we don't even look at them. We shout, "Go away!" and walk away, without even giving them a gentle glance.

There was a disciple who didn't like giving alms. His spiritual master knew this and went to his house, disguised as a beggar. He arrived as the disciple was busy offering milk and fruits in front of a picture of the master. The master begged for some food, but the disciple drove him away, shouting, "There's nothing here for you!" The master then removed his disguise. The disciple was devastated and prostrated at the master's feet.

We are all like that disciple. We love only the external. We don't love the inner essence. We offer milk and *payasam* (a sweet rice dish) to a picture, but not even a penny to the beggar! Amma doesn't mean that we should lavish money on beggars. We have to be careful when we give people money because many will spend it on alcohol or drugs. Instead, we can give food, clothes, and a few kind words. That is our duty to God. So, my children, feed those who are hungry and help those who are suffering.

God is everywhere, pervading everything. What can we offer to God? Real love and devotion for God is nothing other than being compassionate towards the poor and those in need.

My children, this is Amma's message to you: Comfort the grieving and assist the poor. To chase away the poor or to hiss at them is not a sign of devotion. No amount of prayer will bear fruit if it is done while harming or speaking ill of others. Let us say a few consoling words to those who come to us. Let us welcome them with a smile. Get rid of any arrogance and be humble. Even if there is some error on the part of others, be forgiving to the utmost extent. These are different aspects of prayer. Such prayers are accepted by God.

Even if we chant our mantra a million times and go on countless pilgrimages, we won't attain God if we harbor ill will towards others or trample them underfoot. The only result of milk poured into an unwashed pot is that the milk will be spoiled. Good actions purify the mind.

My children, Amma is asking you – not ordering you, because Amma doesn't have the power to order anyone – to take a vow to give up a bad habit or an article of luxury. There is no other way to make our prayers bear fruit.

Every effort should be made to mould our hearts in such a way that we are ready to help those living in misery and to console the suffering. In order to expand our minds, it is said that the hungry should be given food, not abusive words. We will never forget the face of someone who came to help us when we were in distress.

If our finger accidentally pokes our eye, we don't cut off our finger! We forgive the finger and we caress and comfort the eye, because the eye and the hand are our own. My children, in the same way, we should love others to the utmost extent and forgive their mistakes. This is true love for God. Those who have such love in their hearts will receive God's grace.

Some people come to Amma and say, "Amma, I have all these problems. Please make a *sankalpa* (divine resolve) for me!" But as soon as they've crossed to the mainland on the ashram ferry, we see those same people heading straight for the liquor store. Others are even drunk when they come here. Amma isn't angry at them, nor does she question their rights. Amma even makes a sankalpa for them, but they are unable to receive the benefit. Their minds are like rocks. Their lives are full of selfishness.

Prayer

You may visit the *ashram* for many years, receive Amma's darshan and pray countless times, but to derive any real benefit from this, you also have to perform good actions. When you come here, you can unload the burdens of your mind. However, some of those who come here are concerned only about going back home as soon as possible. What kind of surrender is this?

Amma usually feels sorry seeing the grief of her children. But for some people her heart doesn't melt because her mind says, "That person is selfish. See how much money and energy he or she is spending on illusory things. Why should Amma make a resolve for those who are not ready to forgo even one selfish thing?" This is the reason why some people don't get what they wish for. How can Amma shower her compassion on those who lead completely selfish lives?

What makes Amma's *sankalpa* bear fruit are her children's prayers and good deeds. Without these, her children won't receive any benefit even if Amma makes a resolve for them. The TV station broadcasts programs, but we can see those programs only if we tune our TV sets properly. Likewise, you have to tune your mind to the world of God in order to get any benefit.

Try to take at least one step towards the Supreme Being. Then you will see how many steps the Supreme Being takes towards you! Those who do give up selfishness, do good deeds, and pray in the right way won't have to face any sorrow. Haven't you heard the story of Kuchela?[5] These aren't just stories; they are true experiences. And how many countless such experiences there are!

---

[5] See glossary

My children, you should pray with love and devotion. Your hearts should melt as you pray. Tears are sometimes considered to be a weakness. But shedding tears for the vision of God is not a weakness at all. The brilliance of the candle increases as it melts down. Tears are an easy way to make the mind more expansive. Our tears wash away the impurities of the mind, and we gain strength from this.

On the other hand, crying is a weakness when we cry for things that are unreal; it just drains our strength. Shedding tears out of anxiety for the things to be gained tomorrow is weakness. And, then, when the time comes to achieve something, you have lost all your strength from weeping and you get sick.

If you suffer an injury, apply the proper medicine. It is useless to just go on weeping. Some parents are overcome with anxiety about arranging marriages for their children. Unable to sleep, the parents resort to sleeping pills, and on the wedding day the mother or father is in the hospital. Amma sees countless weak-minded people like this. Some worry about building a house. By the time the house is finally built, the owner can't even walk around the house, because he or she has had a heart attack. Most people today lose their enthusiasm, energy, and health owing to anxiety about numerous things such as these. This is weakness. On the other hand, when we shed tears for God, we gain enthusiasm, energy, and peace.

The purpose of having faith in God and praying is not to attain a heaven after death. Some people say that spiritual masters and ashrams foster superstition and are only for the deluded. But those who make such claims do not understand the truth; they lack intelligence. It is their minds that are out of shape. The spiritual masters teach us how we can transcend the weaknesses of the mind, and how we can make sure the harmony of life isn't disturbed. Ashrams are centers that impart these teachings.

Steel rods are used in construction work to reinforce concrete. Without them, buildings would collapse. Faith in God can be compared to those rods. Faith strengthens our feeble minds. If we have faith, we don't cry for illusory things or end up going crazy over them.

In the newspapers you can read that many people commit suicide every day. The reason for most of those deaths has nothing to do with health or wealth; it has to do with lack of mental strength. Such mental weakness will disappear if we can develop real faith in God. With faith, the mind becomes quiet. We are then able to overcome minor difficulties without succumbing to them.

So, my children, take total refuge in the Supreme, in God. Be the owner of a good mind and then you won't have to be sad; everything you need will come to you. If this doesn't happen, tell Amma about it! It won't fail to happen. Amma is talking from her own long experience.

Practice moderation

Most of Amma's children who come here are preoccupied with the thought of going back home once they reach here. They are worried about taking the bus. As soon as they meet Amma, they are in a hurry to prostrate and rush back. Many of them have only one thing to say: "Amma, there's no one at home, so we have to leave right away. It's soon time for the bus to leave." Surrender is not something verbal; it is shown in our actions. Those children are unable to surrender completely to the Supreme Truth, even for that one day when they are here. Even if they meet Amma, rare indeed are those who seek the path to God in the midst of all the complaints and requests they place before her. This doesn't mean that we should ignore worldly matters, but we should recognize that they are not permanent. My children, even though we may have chased after worldly things all these days, forgoing food or sleep, it has yielded only sorrow. Don't forget this. So, from now on, when you visit a temple or an ashram, dedicate a little of your time entirely to God. Put aside your attachments, at least during that time.

There was once a king who decided to leave his throne and enter the life of a vanaprastha.[6] He decided to give all of his wealth to his subjects. He gave whatever each person asked for. A young man came before the king and described his problems. The king gave him a substantial amount of wealth, but the young man wasn't satisfied. His wife had told him as he set out for the palace, "Come back only after you have been given as much as possible by the king!" Seeing the man's greed, the king said, "There is a river here in which precious coral grows, and you can make it your own." The young man was thrilled. The king continued, "But there is one condition. You will be given exactly twelve hours. Take a boat and row as far as you can and return within that time. You can claim the part of the river that you have traversed, and all the coral found there will be yours. But if you are late by even a second, you'll get nothing." The young man agreed. On the appointed day, crowds of people gathered on both banks of the river to watch him row. His wife and friends urged him to claim ownership of the entire river, no matter how hard it was to achieve. They reminded him of what a great accomplishment it would be to become the owner of so much wealth. The man was excited and started rowing. He rowed for six hours; and, then, because of his greed, he decided to continue going forward. Two more hours passed. Now there were only four hours left to return to the starting point. In half the time, he had to cover all the distance he had traveled in eight hours. He started rowing very fast. His wife and friends encouraged him and prodded him

---

[6] Traditionally, in India, there are four stages of life. Vanaprastha is the third stage of life. When a couple's children are old enough to take care of themselves, the parents retreat to a hermitage or an ashram, where they live a purely spiritual life, doing spiritual practice.

on. They called out, "Your efforts will be totally wasted if you are late by even a second! Hurry up! Row fast!" The time was almost up. But it was a long way back to the starting point. He rowed with all his might. His chest began to hurt. Still, he didn't stop rowing. He pressed one hand against his chest and kept on rowing with the other. His fatigue grew. He vomited blood, and yet he didn't stop rowing because of his greed for more wealth. Finally, he managed to get back to the starting point one second before the appointed time. His wife and friends danced with joy. But the young man collapsed and breathed his last right there.

Now the wife faced the problem of taking the body back home. Home was far away. Some kind of conveyance was needed. The wife said, "Anyway, he's dead. I would have to rent a vehicle if I were to bring the body back home. I have to bring up our children; I don't have enough money to rent any transportation, so let us bury him somewhere here! That will be enough." So, for the young man, it all ended six feet beneath the ground. No one accompanied him. His wife and friends, who had urged him on to get all that undeserved wealth, and his children – none of them came with him. Nor did any of the wealth. This is life, my children! People live their lives without giving their minds even a moment of peace. They constantly worry about their family and wealth, and often resort to unscrupulous means to gain worldly riches. But does anything accompany them in the end? No.

Suffering begins the moment desires for worldly things arise. Even if the desires are satisfied, suffering is just waiting its turn because the things we desire are not permanent. They will be lost tomorrow, if not today. God is the only source of permanent peace. You can avoid suffering if you recognize that material pleasures do not last and you begin to live accordingly.

Amma isn't saying that you don't need wealth or worldly objects. Let there be enough of that to meet your needs in life, but not more. Be aware of what is everlasting and gives you peace, and strive to gain that. Heaven and hell exist here on earth. It is the mind that creates either heaven or hell. So, the mind needs to be controlled. Then we won't have to experience sorrow. There will be only bliss, bliss, and bliss.

Amma looking at her children during her birthday celebration

True devotion: devotion to the God principle

Amma's birthday message 1991

My children, close your eyes and calm your minds. Let go of all thoughts and concentrate on the feet of your beloved deity. Don't think of your home or work or catching the bus back home. Think only about your beloved deity. Give up all talk and chant God's name. It doesn't matter how much water you pour on the branches of a tree; doing so is useless. But if you pour water at the roots, it will reach all parts of the tree. So, focus only on God's feet, for to think of anything else is as useless as pouring water on the tree branches.

If your boat is tied to the river bank, you won't be able to get across the river, no matter how hard you row. Similarly, when you pray, if your mind is tied to your family and wealth, you won't get the proper benefit of your prayers, no matter how much you pray. So, when you pray, let your mind be totally surrendered to God. My children, only this will bear fruit.

In the world of spirituality, there is no birth or death. The day the concept that we are born disappears, we have reached God's door. The realm of the Supreme Being lies beyond both life and death.

Amma has agreed to these celebrations only with the happiness of her children in mind. This is the time when your renunciation, love, and sense of equality become manifest. Furthermore, Amma gets a chance to see all of you together.

Those who have come here shouldn't go back having done nothing. Go home only after repeating a mantra and meditating for a little while. Spiritual practice is our only true wealth, and this is why Amma asks you to do archana.[7]

Because Amma gives great importance to prayer, there are those who belittle our path as one of devotion (*bhakti*). They view devotion as inferior. Some people deny the existence of God. For others, God is formless and attributeless. Such people usually see devotion as a weakness. It is true that worshipping many different gods or evil spirits is nothing but blind devotion. Real devotion teaches us to see the one, all-pervading Supreme Being within ourselves and in everything.

There was a man who was hailed by everyone as a man of devotion. Early one morning, one of his friends came to see him. But the visitor was told that the man was busy worshipping Lord Ganesha. After a while, the visitor enquired again and learned that his friend was now doing *puja* (a sacred ritual) to Lord Shiva. The visitor went and dug a pit in the courtyard. After some time, he enquired again. His friend was now worshipping the Divine Mother. The visitor dug another pit. When the host finally emerged having performed all the different *pujas*, he noticed that his courtyard was full of holes. He asked his friend what had happened. His friend replied, "I wanted some water. If I had used the time I spent digging all these separate holes to dig in just one place, I would have found plenty of water long ago. Now, all I have to show for digging all these holes is a waste of time and energy!" The devotee understood what his friend was implying. If the time he spent on worshipping numerous gods had been used to focus his mind on just one deity, he would have attained his goal long ago. All gods are the one God that dwells within us. The man gave up his immature, primitive devotion and became a true devotee.

---

[7] A form of worship in which the names of a deity are chanted, usually 108, 300 or 1000 times in one sitting.

Prayer has its unique place in spiritual practice. Prayer is not a weakness. If we pray with faith and sincerity, we can awaken the love that lies dormant within us. This can be compared to the technique of catching fish by shining a light into the water.

Devotion is actually the discrimination (*viveka*) between the eternal and the transitory. The actions we perform with the awareness of what is everlasting and what is perishable is devotion.

There is another reason why devotion is important. We can make rapid progress with our spiritual practice by following the same pattern we have followed so far in life. In childhood, we find happiness sitting in our mother's lap. A little later, we find happiness in sharing our pleasures and sorrows with our friends. When we grow up, a husband or wife arrives to share our sorrows. Thus, we tend to keep our minds centered on some person or other as we move through each stage of life. That is how people find happiness. Such minds may not be able to rise suddenly to the level worshipping a formless Supreme Being, so worshipping God with a form is more practical.

Even if we convince ourselves intellectually that God has no form or attributes, we forget this as different situations arise. There was a man who used to keep his ink bottle on the left side of his desk, and whenever he wrote he dipped his pen into the ink. One day he moved the ink bottle to the right side of the desk. Even though he knew the bottle was to his right, his hand automatically moved to the left to dip the pen, because that long practice had become part of his nature. Similarly, each of our habits devours us. Habits can't be changed quickly.

For years, we've been used to leaning on something. But, continuing to depend on habitual patterns of behavior can actually be helpful to our spiritual practice; it can be easier to gain inner purity this way than by any other method. This is why Amma advises that you take refuge in your beloved deity as you proceed through life. Free the mind from its attachment to wealth, family, friends, position, fame, etc., and attach the mind only to God. Redirect your present attachment and devotion to all those things towards God instead.

By chanting the mantra of your beloved deity, you can reduce the number of thoughts in your mind from one hundred to ten. As you chant more and more, the mind will quiet down and become crystal clear.

Just as you can see the sun reflected clearly on the surface of a waveless lake, you can see the form of the Supreme Being clearly in your mind when it is absolutely quiet. This isn't a path of weakness, nor is it primitive. It is a shortcut to the ultimate goal.

Amma doesn't insist that you follow a particular path. You have the freedom to choose any path. Don't think that one path is different from or superior to another. All paths lead to one and the same Truth. All paths should be respected.

Iddli, dosha and *puttu*[8] are different dishes, but they're all made of rice. We can choose what best suits our taste and digestive powers. Every one of those dishes will appease our hunger. Similarly, people belong to different cultures and have different tastes. The spiritual masters have indicated different paths to suit different tastes. Even though the paths may appear to be different, their essence is the same and they all lead to the same goal.

Service, the passport to God

Amma sees much change in her children compared to last year. Several of you have given up smoking, drinking, and luxuries. But not all of you have done this. Next year Amma wants to see these changes in twice as many of you. That would be a real birthday present!

---

[8] Traditional Indian dishes.

There are some of you who have come here from far away places; you've had to catch several buses and go through a lot of trouble to reach the ashram. But, even so, you don't seem to have the patience to stay here even for a moment. There are others who, once they reach here, are interested in gossiping and smoking. Some people even arrive here drunk. My children, when you come to the ashram, having spent your money for this and taking all that trouble, you should come here to focus on God. During the time you are here, you should try to turn the mind inward, meditating and repeating your mantra in solitude. My dear children, you should have the attitude of prayer and doing selfless service. You have to drive away your primitive selfishness.

You know that bliss doesn't reside in objects; bliss is within you. When we depend on external objects for our happiness, we lose our strength. Real happiness doesn't come from such things. If true happiness could be found in alcohol or drugs, there wouldn't be any reason for people who use them to end up in mental hospitals. Because they think that happiness is to be found outside, they always end up crying in sorrow. Those who smoke can clearly see the warning on the cigarette packets: "Smoking is injurious to your health." Yet, even after reading those words, they light a cigarette and smoke! They have become slaves to their habit. They are weak. A courageous person stands firm on his or her own strength. To be dependent on other things is not a sign of courage; it is slavery. Those who are worried about what others may think if they don't smoke or drink are the worst type of cowards and weaklings.

My dear children, so many destitute people struggle for their next meal or a change of clothes. Countless children drop out of school because they have no way of paying the fees. Many poor people live in houses with leaking roofs because they don't have the means to construct a new roof. And there are so many who suffer and are writhing in pain because they can't afford to buy the medicines that could alleviate their pain. The money people spend on alcohol and drugs, which completely ruin their health and their lives, would be sufficient to help the poor who are suffering.

The compassion that you show the suffering – that is your true love for Amma. Cultivate an attitude of serving others, even sacrificing your own comforts in order to do so. Then, God will come running to you and embrace you.

My children, it isn't possible to attain God through prayer alone. You can't be cleared for the journey to Liberation without the passport of selfless service. Only those who do selfless deeds are qualified to attain God, to attain the Goal of Liberation.

Constant practice is essential

Amma knows that despite her repeated statements that bliss is within you, and is not something to be found externally, you cannot fully absorb this truth until you experience it.

A mother and her son lived in a mouse-infested house. The son began thinking of ways to kill all the mice. First he considered getting a cat, but then he decided that a mouse trap would be more suitable. He didn't have enough money to buy a mouse trap, so he decided to build one himself. He began to prepare the materials for it. While engaged in the work, the boy suddenly began to feel that he, himself, was turning into a mouse! This feeling became very strong. He began to tremble with fear as he imagined himself being caught by a cat. His mother noticed that he was panicking and asked what was wrong. He said, "The cat is coming!" "So what?" asked his mother. The terrified boy replied, "I am a mouse! If the cat sees me, he'll eat me!" Again and again, his mother tried to reassure him, saying, "Son, you are definitely not a mouse!" But his fear remained and he kept insisting he was a mouse. Finally she took him to a doctor. The doctor said, "You are not a mouse. Look at me. Look at these people. How are you different from them?" He made the boy stand in front of a mirror, and the boy's fear disappeared. The boy walked home with his mother. As they neared their home, a cat ran across the road. As soon as he saw the cat, the boy's mood changed. He cried, "Oh no! There's a cat!" – and he ran and hid behind a tree. His mother took him straight back to the doctor. The doctor said, "Didn't I explain to you that you are a human being and not a mouse? So, how can you still be scared when you see a cat?" The boy replied, "Doctor, I know that I'm a human and that I'm not a mouse. But the cat doesn't know that!"

My children, no matter how long we study the scriptures, regardless of how many times we say to ourselves that we have the strength to overcome any problem, if we haven't brought our minds fully under control we will still falter when faced with difficulties. We may hear countless times that we are not the body, mind, or intellect, that we are the embodiments of bliss, but we forget this when we encounter even trivial problems. Constant practice is therefore essential if we want to be strong in the face of difficulties. We need to train the mind to remain in that awareness continuously. The mind should be trained to push away all obstacles from our path with the conviction that we are not lambs but lion cubs! We should surrender to God no matter what sorrows befall us, and perform our actions fearlessly. It is so much better to surrender everything at God's feet and to courageously engage in action than to waste our time and ruin our health grieving. Circumstances cannot be changed by succumbing to sorrow or lamenting aloud. So why indulge in sadness? If there's a wound, we have to put a healing salve on it instead of just weeping. In the same way, what is required in any crisis is to seek a remedy without faltering.

My children, if you can't completely control your sadness, meditate and chant a mantra for a short while or read some scriptural text. Tie the mind down to some task that you like instead of letting it wander. Your mind will then quiet down. In this way, you won't waste time or ruin your health.

When a car or a building is insured, the owner is free from worry, knowing that if some accident should occur, the insurance company will reimburse for damages. Similarly, those who perform actions with their minds surrendered to the Supreme do not need to fear. In any crisis, God will be there to help us. He will protect and guide us.

How to give charity

My children, feeling compassion for the poor, feeling our hearts melt because of the pain of others, should be our inspiration to serve. If we work a little longer even when we feel exhausted, that effort, offered selflessly without expecting anything in return, will show our sense of dedication to our work. If the money we may receive from this is used to help the poor, it will be a sign of our compassion. My children, prayer alone isn't enough. We have to perform good actions as well.

To get a job, educational qualifications are not sufficient; we also need a character reference. We won't get *payasam* by just pouring rice into a pot of water and boiling it; we have to add brown sugar and grated coconut. Only by combining the right ingredients do we get *payasam*. Similarly, prayer alone won't make us eligible for divine grace. Selfless service, renunciation, surrender, and compassion are all essential.

There was once a man who, even though very wealthy, had no peace of mind. He thought that if he could only reach heaven, he would always be happy, and he sought the advice of many people on how to attain heaven. Finally, he came across a monk who said to him, "By giving charity you can reach heaven. But you shouldn't feel any judgment towards the recipients of your charity, and your money should be given liberally." The rich man bought many cows, which he planned to give away. He didn't have to spend much money because he purchased old cows that nobody else wanted to buy. The monk had told him not to count the cash he gave away. He therefore changed some money into small coins, so that it wouldn't amount to much when he gave away handfuls. The date of the charitable event was advertised beforehand. The monk knew the rich man quite well. He was worried that the man's actions, done in the hope of gaining heaven, would instead lead him to hell, and he decided to try to save him. He disguised himself as a beggar and joined the line of people waiting to receive the charitable donations. He received a handful of coins and a cow that was no more than a bundle of bones, too feeble to walk. When he had received those things, the monk presented the rich man with a golden bowl. The rich man was overjoyed to think that he had received something in return that was much more valuable than what he had given! The disguised monk said to the man, "I have a request to make. Please return that bowl to me when we get to heaven!" The rich man was dumbfounded. "Return it to you when we get to heaven! How will that be possible? We have to die before we get to heaven. So, how can we take all those things with us? Once we die, none of these objects will come with us!"

The rich man began to think about what he himself had just said, that nothing will accompany us beyond the threshold of death. And wisdom dawned in his mind. He thought, "When we die, we cannot take any riches with us. Then why am I being so miserly towards those poor people?

What a sinner I am to have been so stingy!" The rich man fell at the feet of the holy man who had opened his eyes. He begged forgiveness for the wrongs he had done to his fellow beings. He gave away his wealth without a trace of regret. As he did this, he experienced a bliss he had never felt before in his life.

My children, even though many of us give presents to others, most of us are stingy in our giving. Remember this, my children: no matter how rich we may be, none of our treasures will be with us forever. So why be stingy? We should do as much as we possibly can to help the suffering. This is true wealth. This is the path to peace and tranquility.

My children, we should surrender our minds to God. This is not easy because the mind is not an object we can just pick up and give away. However, when we surrender something the mind is attached to, it is the same as surrendering the mind. At present, most people's minds are attached to wealth more than to anything else, even more than to their loved ones. There are many who, knowing that they will get their share of the family property only after the death of their parents, are even ready to do away with their parents in some way or another! And if they find out that their share of the property will be smaller than expected, they may file a suit against their parents! Their love for the property is stronger than their love for their parents.

When we give up the wealth to which our minds are attached, we are actually surrendering our minds. Only the prayers flowing from a heart that has developed this attitude of surrender will bear fruit. God has no need for our wealth or prestige. The sun doesn't need the light of a candle. We are the ones who profit from our own surrender. Through our surrender we become fit for God's grace. We can then enjoy bliss forever. Our worldly wealth will definitely vanish sooner or later. But if we install God in its place, we become the owners of everlasting joy.

Small things can rob us of our mental control. As a result, we lose our concentration when we work, and we are unable to show our family and friends any love. Gradually, we develop bitterness and hatred towards everything in life. We lose sleep because of our lack of inner peace. We reach a stage in which we can't sleep without the aid of pills. How many such examples can be seen around us! With real faith in God, meditation, mantra repetition, and prayer, we can gain enough strength to meet any situation without faltering. We will then be able to do anything with our full attention, whether the circumstances are favorable or not. So, my children, without wasting any time, chant your mantra and perform your actions selflessly. These are the things that lead us to peace and harmony.

See only good in everything

My children, if you really love God, you have to stop your fault-finding. God will never dwell in a fault-finding mind. Try not to find fault with anyone. Remember that it is only because there are faults in us that we see faults in others.

There was once a king who asked each of his subjects to create a sculpture and bring it to him. On the appointed day, many people came to his palace with their sculptures. The king asked his minister to judge each sculpture and award a prize according to its merit. But the minister didn't have a single nice thing to say about any of the sculptures! According to him, each one had one or several defects. He said to the king, "Not one of your subjects has made a praiseworthy work of art." The minister's words displeased the king, who gravely replied, "Every one of those people created something according to his or her ability and knowledge. It is true that none of them created a masterpiece, and we have to keep this in mind when we evaluate their work. Nothing in this world can be called perfect or complete; everything will always have some defect. But the fact that you couldn't find a single sculpture that had some quality worthy of being awarded a small prize tells me that you are not qualified to be a minister!" The king relieved the minister of his job. So, the one who could see only faults in others lost his job. My children, there is bound to be some goodness in everything, but we need the eyes to see this.

When those who try to see only the good in others chant a mantra just once, they derive the benefit equivalent to chanting the mantra ten million times. Amma's heart melts when she thinks of such people. God will bring them whatever they need.

Become one in Love
Amma's birthday message 1992

My children, the soul has no birth or death. Even the thought that we are born should die. The purpose of being born as a human being is to realize this. You may ask, if this is so, why has Amma agreed to this celebration? Well, because it makes Amma happy to see all of you here together. It gives Amma the opportunity to see all of you sit together and chant the divine mantra. Group chanting is especially important. It will also make all of you happy if your desire to celebrate this day is fulfilled. It gives Amma joy to see her children happy. Furthermore, today is the day of renunciation. Here you don't have the comforts you enjoy at home. You work ceaselessly in Amma's name without food or sleep. You engage yourselves in work that gives solace and peace to the suffering. My children, these are the actions that awaken the Self (*Atman*).

It is true that we could help a lot of poor people with the money that is spent on these celebrations. But in today's circumstances we cannot just get rid of these kinds of celebrations. We add copper to pure gold to make it suitable for making ornaments. To uplift people, one has to empathize with them. My children, if there is any mistake on Amma's part, please forgive Amma!

My children, earlier all of you chanted *Om Amriteshwaryai Namah*. My children, that goddess is the essence of the nectar of the Immortal Self (*atmamrita*), which resides in the thousand-petaled lotus at the crown of your head. That is what you have to attain, and not this five-foot body. Discover your own inner power. Discover the bliss within yourself. This is the true meaning of the chant.

Pray for devotion

My children, once you develop love for God, you won't be able to think of anything else. If people complain, saying, "For how many years have I been going to the temple to do puja and to call upon God! And yet I have never, at any time, been free from sorrow!" – all Amma will say to such people is that they haven't really called upon God at all, because their minds were filled with other things. Those who love God know no sorrow. There is only bliss in the lives of those who are fully immersed in their love for God. Where do such people get the time to think of their own sorrows or other problems? Everywhere and in everything they see only their beloved deity. If we pray to God, it should be only for the sake of loving God, and not to gain material things. When Amma thinks of love for God, the story of Vidura's wife comes to mind. Both Vidura and his wife were ardent devotees of Lord Krishna. Vidura once invited Lord Krishna to his house. He and his wife waited anxiously for the day of the Lord's visit. They thought of nothing but Krishna. They were thinking about how to receive him, what to offer him, what they were going to say to him, and so on. Finally, the day arrived. They made all the preparations for the Lord's visit. The time of Krishna's arrival drew close. Vidura's wife went to take a bath before the Lord arrived. It was while she was taking a bath that Krishna arrived, earlier than expected. A maid came and informed her of the Lord's arrival. Vidura's wife ran out, calling, "Krishna! Krishna!" and approached the Lord. She had forgotten that she had just been having her bath. She brought fruits for the Lord and prepared a seat for him. And as she did these things she was continuously chanting, "Krishna! Krishna!" In her state of devotion, she wasn't aware of anything else. She ended up sitting down on the seat meant for the Lord, while he sat on the floor!

She wasn't aware of any of this. She peeled a banana. She threw away the fruit, and lovingly offered the peel to the Lord! He sat there smiling and relished the peel. It was then that Vidura came into the room. He was dismayed at the scene. His wife was sitting stark naked and dripping wet on Krishna's seat, while the Lord was made to sit on the floor!

He couldn't believe his eyes. She was throwing away the banana and feeding Krishna with the peel! And Krishna was enjoying all this as if nothing strange were happening.

Vidura was furious. "Oh, you wicked one, what do you think you're doing!" he shouted at his wife. It was only then that she returned to her senses and became aware of what she had done. She ran out of the room, and after a while she returned wearing newly washed clothes. She and Vidura made the Lord sit in his chair and they worshipped his holy feet as they had planned. They offered him the numerous delicacies they had prepared. She selected a beautiful banana, carefully peeled it, and offered it to him. When it was all over, Krishna said, "Even though you performed all of those rituals exactly according to tradition, they couldn't equal the reception I received when I first arrived! What you gave me later didn't match the taste of the banana peel I first received!" The reason was that Vidura's wife had completely forgotten herself in her devotion while she offered him the banana peel.

My children, this is the kind of devotion that is needed. We should forget ourselves in the presence of God. Then there is no longer any duality, no 'you' or 'I.' And, then, there is no need for rituals. All rituals are meant to help us get rid of our sense of duality. So, this kind of love is what we need to have towards God. There shouldn't be any room in our hearts for anything other than God. A river is bound by two banks, but the river bed is one and the same. Likewise, even though we speak of God and the devotee, or of the master and the disciple, it is love that takes us to the uniting principle of the Self. So, my children, your prayer to God should be, "Make me love You, and let me forget everything else!" This is the lasting wealth of life, the wellspring of bliss. If we develop such devotion, we have succeeded in life.

Compassion – the first step in spirituality

My children, when Amma talks of the need for devotion towards God, she doesn't mean just prayer. Love for God doesn't just mean sitting somewhere and crying for God. We should be able to perceive God's presence in every living being. Our smile and our loving kindness towards others also reveal our love and devotion for God. When we open our hearts to God in devotion, these things happen spontaneously. Then we won't be angry or unloving towards anyone.

A poor man fell ill and was unable to work. He had nothing to eat for a few days and became very weak. He approached several people and begged for some food, but no one paid him any attention. He knocked on many doors, but everyone drove him away. The poor man became extremely despondent. He felt that he didn't want to live in a world where people were so cruel, and he decided to put an end to his life. But he was very hungry. He thought, "If only I could appease my hunger, I would die in peace." He decided to ask for food just one more time. He went to a hut where a woman lived. To his surprise, she lovingly asked him to sit down and went inside the hut to get him some food. But in the hut she discovered that the pot containing the food was lying upside down. The cat had knocked it over and had eaten the food. She returned outside and with great sadness said to the man, "I'm so sorry! I had some rice and vegetables in the house that I was hoping to give to you, but the cat ate it. There's nothing left. I cannot give you any money either because I don't have any. Please forgive me for disappointing you like this!" The man replied, "But you have given me what I needed. I was sick. I begged many people for food, but everyone drove me away. Not one of them had even a kind word for me. I felt I couldn't live in a world like that and had decided to commit suicide. But I couldn't bear the hunger, so I decided to try one more place. And that is why I came here. Even though I didn't get any food, your words of love have filled me with happiness. It is because there are kind souls like you in this world that poor people like myself are given the courage to live. Thanks to you I am not going to kill myself. Today I feel happy and contented for the first time I can remember."

My children, even if we have nothing material to give away, surely we can offer others a smile or a kind word. That doesn't cost us much, does it? A kind heart is enough – that is the first step on the spiritual path. A person who does this need not go anywhere in search of God. God will come running to the heart that is full of compassion. That is God's dearest dwelling place. My children, a person who has no compassion for his or her fellow beings cannot be called a devotee.

All of you, my children, have come here today. When you were here last year, you made a vow. Most of you have kept your vows. Many of you have stopped drinking and smoking, and have given up luxuries. This year, as well – if you love Amma, and if you feel any compassion for the world – you should make a similar vow to give up your bad habits. Think of how much money we waste on alcohol, cigarettes, expensive clothes, and luxuries! My children, you should try your utmost to reduce your purchases of such things. The money you will save in this way can be used to help the poor. There are very intelligent children who have to interrupt their education because they cannot afford to pay college fees. You can help them by paying their fees. You can help the homeless. And there are so many sick people who are suffering because they can't afford to buy the medicines they need. You can buy them medicines. There are many different ways in which we can help others. The money we are wasting now would be enough to help others. Serving those in need is true worship of God. This is the type of *pada puja*[9] that makes Amma happy and contented. Let us pray to the Almighty to make our hearts compassionate.

[9] The worship of God's, the Guru's, or a saint's feet.

Mother Nature protects
those who protect Her

Amma's birthday message 1993

The devotees who assembled in Amritapuri from all parts of the world to celebrate Amma's fortieth birthday wished to feel blessed by performing a pada puja to her on that auspicious day. In the gloomy atmosphere created by an earthquake that had just taken place in Midwestern India, Amma was very reluctant to agree to a pada puja or any other type of celebration. She finally yielded to the heartfelt prayers of her children. At eight in the morning, Amma arrived on the dais at the southern end of the spacious pandal (traditional tent-like structure) that had been constructed in the ashram compound. After a very beautiful, deeply devotional pada puja, Amma wanted to console the crowd of devotees who had been unable to find a comfortable place to sit in the pandal. She said, "My children, try to sit wherever you can find a space. Amma knows that not all of you could find a convenient spot. Please don't feel unhappy about that, my children! Amma's mind is also very close to those children who are standing far away. There is a slight drizzle, so we will soon go inside the hall." Amma then began her birthday message.

My children, accepting this *puja* today is the greatest mistake of Amma's life. Amma said a hundred times that there was no need for a *puja*. She should be serving you instead, because that is where Amma's happiness lies. She is sitting here only to make you happy. During the US Tour [two months earlier] Amma said that there would be no need for any celebrations during her birthday this year.

There was a sadness in Amma's heart. Just think of today's situation! Rotting corpses and thousands of grieving survivors. There is no way to protect the survivors or to cremate the dead.

There are not enough people to help. Amma wants to hasten to that place. She has already asked some of her children to go there. Think of all the people there, suffering from the loss of their dear ones and their possessions!

This situation is not specific to India; in one way or another it's happening everywhere. Amma isn't thinking about those who have died. They are gone. But there are thousands who are suffering and in pain. Amma is worried about them. Those are the ones we need to save. It is their security we have to ensure. My children, you should make an effort in this direction.

Protect Nature

Why is the earth inflicting all this pain on us? Think about it, my children. Think of how much sacrifice Mother Nature makes, and the great sacrifices the rivers, trees, and animals make for us! Look at a tree. It gives us fruit, shade, and coolness; it gives shade even to someone who is cutting it down. This is the attitude of the trees. In the same way, we can examine everything in nature and observe how it makes a tremendous sacrifice for humanity. But what are *we* doing for nature? It is said that we should plant a sapling whenever we cut down a tree. But how many people follow that advice? And even if they do, how can the harmony of nature be maintained with a sapling? A small sapling cannot give nature the same strength that a large tree gives. Can a small child do the work of an adult? While the adult carries a whole basket of earth, the child carries a small spoonful. There is a great difference.

To clean a drum of water, is it enough to add just one milligram of water-purifier instead of the prescribed ten? This is the condition of nature conservation today. Nature is losing her harmony. The cool, gentle breeze that should caress us has turned into a huge tornado. The earth that has been our support until today is now dragging us into hell.

But this isn't nature's fault. We are reaping the fruits of our own unrighteousness. It is like the man who earns his living selling coffins and ultimately ends up inside one of his own creations. We are digging our own graves. Everyone is scared now. We go to bed at night, uncertain about whether we will wake up in the morning. My children, protecting nature should be our first priority. Only then do we have a chance to survive. We have to stop destroying nature for the sake of money, for our own selfish ends. At the same time, all of you should try to plant trees on at least a small patch of land near your homes.

The ancient sages told us to worship trees. In this way they taught us the importance of conserving nature. Growing flowers for worship in our yards, picking those flowers and offering them to God, lighting an oil lamp made of bronze – all of this purifies the atmosphere. Today the air is no longer permeated with the fragrance of flowers or the scent of a wick burning in an oil lamp. What we have instead is the stench of poisonous smoke from the factories. If long ago the human life span was 120 years, it has now shrunk to 60 or 80 years. And there are more and more new diseases. Those diseases are attributed to 'viruses,' but no one knows their real cause. The atmosphere is polluted, diseases are on the rise, our health is being ruined, and our life spans are being reduced – this is the way we are proceeding. We try to create heaven on earth, but instead this earth is being turned into hell. We want to eat sweet things, but we can't because of illness. At night we want to watch a dance performance, but we can't stay awake, again because of illness. In this way, humans are unable to satisfy their desires in life. Humanity cannot unravel the knot it has tied. Hardly anyone thinks about how all of this will end or how to solve the situation. Even if someone thinks of a solution, nothing is put into practice.

When we grow flowering plants, pick the flowers, and offer them to God, both our hearts and nature are purified. The devotee chants a mantra while watering the plant, picking the flowers, making a garland. Chanting a mantra decreases the number of thoughts in the mind, and the mind is purified. But nowadays people dismiss all of this as superstition. We put our faith in perishable, human-made things, such as computers and TVs. We no longer trust the words of the enlightened sages. When the computer or the car develops a problem, people are prepared to work hard for as long as it takes to repair it or to wait for the repairs to be completed. But what are we doing to remove the disharmony of the mind?

Center for training the mind

My children, if the mind is balanced and in tune, everything will be in harmony and in tune. If the mind loses its balance, everything in life will be out of tune. Ashrams are centers where people can be trained in such a way that no disharmony occurs. But nowadays there are people who are inclined to malign and ridicule ashrams and spiritual life.

Recently a film was released in which ashrams in general were ridiculed. Some devotees were upset when they heard the remarks of those who had seen the film. The devotees complained about people who voice opinions without bothering to find out the truth. There is no history of *ganja* (hashish) being seized from any ashram in Kerala. People are ready to blindly believe some fictional account, some grandmother's tale, written for a fictional movie; and they dismiss the words of the *mahatmas* (great souls). Those people proudly call themselves intellectuals. They don't put their faith in what they themselves can see at an ashram, but in the fabricated stories put forth in a movie. Many people have started maligning ashrams after seeing that particular film, but those intellectuals are not willing to enquire about the true situation.

Suppose someone goes up to a person and says to him or her, "I saw you lying dead! I also heard how you died!" – and this is being said to a person who is fully alive! This is what is happening these days. People don't trust what they actually see. What they see in the movies and hear in stories is more important to them. It is part of a story writer's job to take what is in his or her imagination and portray it as real. That is the nature of fictional writing. Writers earn money in this way and become famous. They will write in any manner in order to achieve this. This is how writers and producers make money and live in luxury. But spiritual people are different. Their lives are filled with selflessness.

Amma is not criticizing the arts. The arts are necessary. Every art form has its importance. But the artists should not try to destroy our culture. Art should be created in order to uplift humanity. Art should expand our minds and not turn people into animals. Just because there are a few quack doctors, does it mean that the whole science of medicine is wrong and that all doctors are cheats? To spread such ideas is to betray society. The only works of art that benefit individuals and society are those that teach us how to perceive the good side of everything.

Visitors to this ashram know about the people who live here and are working hard, day and night. They toil, but not so that they may enjoy comforts or give something to their children or families. They work hard for the world. You can see them carrying sand even at midnight to fill the waterlogged land so that they can build a place for our visitors to sleep. It is only because of their hard work, often performed while forsaking food and sleep, that God has made it possible for us to do so much service in such a short time. The householders also do as much selfless service as they can. And we are continuing this even now. Spiritual people in different ashrams have dedicated themselves to serving the world. They don't do anything for their own selfish ends. When young people hear of ashrams nowadays, they think of the ashram of Rajneesh. [10] But his ashram was for western society. He counseled those who were the victims of drugs and other intoxicants. He went down to their level.

When eating oranges, you don't get the same enjoyment out of the seventh orange as you did from the first. You develop an aversion as you continue to experience the same thing, and in this way you come to know that real happiness is not to be found in any object. You will then begin to seek the source of true happiness.

A dog is chewing a bone. When blood oozes, the dog thinks it is coming from the bone. Finally the dog collapses due to all the bleeding. Only then does it realize that the blood isn't coming from the bone but from its own injured gums. This is what the experience of seeking happiness from external things is like.

This is what Rajneesh is also saying. However, his method of teaching is very different from that of the ancient sages. His philosophy is not for the people of India, nor do we agree with his philosophy. But it has to be said that he did everything openly; he didn't hide anything. However, it is difficult to develop detachment by overindulging. Amma isn't saying it is impossible, but the detachment gained through enjoyment is temporary. So we have to consciously cultivate an attitude of detachment towards worldly things. We may like *payasam* (a sweet rice dish), but if we consume a lot of it we'll feel satiated, and later we'll want twice as much. Thus, we can never turn away from sensory pleasures by attempting to satisfy them permanently. Only by consciously adopting an attitude of detachment can we move away from worldly things. This is Amma's way. Today, however, there are many people who

---

[10] Shree Rajneesh (1931-1990), also called Osho, born in Madhya Pradesh in India, had an ashram in Oregon in the US during the 1980s. His teachings were considered controversial.

do not follow this path that was prescribed by our ancient sages; instead, they follow the path prescribed by Rajneesh. And, then, all ashrams are judged on that basis. Those who criticize don't have the eyes to see the hard work and renunciation of the people in Amma's ashram. Even in the West, Amma's western children are working. They cook their own food because it would cost a great deal of money to eat outside. They work hard, save money, and spend it here on selfless service projects. So, we should try to find out the actual truth instead of voicing opinions formed by watching movies and reading magazines.

There are three groups of people in today's world. The first group consists of the poorest people who have nothing. Amma knows many such people who come here. They don't even have one decent piece of clothing, so they come here wearing borrowed clothes. Countless people struggle because they can't afford to thatch their roofs or get treatment when they are ill or pay for an education. They themselves don't know how they manage to survive each day. Then there is the second group of people. They have a little bit of money, which more or less covers their needs. They feel compassion for those who are struggling, but they cannot do anything about it. The third group is different from the first two. They have a hundred times more wealth than they need. They are intelligent; they run businesses and earn a fortune, but they spend their money only to enhance their own comforts and happiness. They don't care about those who are suffering. About them it can be said that they are truly the poorest of the poor. Hell is for them, because they are the cause of the suffering of the destitute. Such people have taken the wealth of the poor and are keeping it for themselves. My children, remember that our duty to God is to be compassionate towards the poor. Devotion is not just going around an image, chanting "Krishna, Mukunda,

Murare!"[11] Real devotion is to help those who are struggling. There are many who wave away or slap the hand that a beggar extends, as if that hand were a fly. Those who have no compassion towards the poor and those in need will not benefit from chanting a mantra or from meditating; for them, no amount of offerings at temples will gain them entry into heaven, and there will be no peace for them in this life.

Sorrow is our own creation

My children, some people ask, "Is God actually biased? Some people are healthy while others are sick, and some people are rich while others are poor. Why is this so?" My children, the fault is not God's; it is ours.

We know what the size of a tomato was in the old days. Today, tomatoes are often more than twice that size because of the contributions made by scientists. Amma isn't rejecting the benefits of science, but when tomatoes become that big their quality decreases. Housewives know that adding baking soda to *iddli*[12] batter makes the *iddlis* larger, but they don't have the quality or taste of normal *iddlis*. Poisons enter our bodies because of the use of artificial fertilizers and other chemicals in the cultivation of tomatoes. Our cells are destroyed. Children born to parents who consume such food are unhealthy from birth itself. We thus suffer the consequences of our own actions. There is no use in blaming God. If our actions are pure, the results will be good. What we experience now is the fruit of our actions in our previous lives.

A man once gave two of his friends a stone slab each. One of his friends was a very healthy man and the other was thin and weak. After a few days, the man asked his friends to break the stones. They began to pound the stones with a hammer. The

---

[11] Different names of Lord Krishna.
[12] South Indian steamed rice cakes.

healthy man hit his stone ten times, but it didn't even crack. The weak man hit his stone just twice and it broke into two pieces. The healthy man said, "You hit the stone only twice and it broke! How did you manage that?" The other man replied, "I had pounded the stone many times beforehand."

Likewise, if life at present is a struggle for some and easy for others, it is the result or fruits of their previous actions. Our success today is the fruit of the good actions we performed yesterday. And if this success is to continue in the future, we have to do good deeds today; otherwise, we will have to experience suffering tomorrow. If we are compassionate towards those who struggle today, we can avoid suffering tomorrow. By helping those who have fallen into a ditch to climb out, we can avoid our own fall tomorrow.

My children, it is difficult to understand through reason or intellect what *prarabdha*[13] is. Only through experience can we learn this. Certain junctures arise in our lives when many obstacles, such as incurable diseases, accidents, untimely death, quarrels, loss of wealth, etc., may crop up. There is no use simply blaming one's *prarabdha* at such times. We can overcome those difficulties through our own effort and with the attitude of surrender. Through meditation and mantra repetition, we can certainly change our *prarabdha*, at least ninety percent of it, but not 100 percent, because it is the law of nature. It affects even the *mahatmas*. But there is a difference, in that nothing really affects such great souls, for they have no attachments within. The suffering that arises from one's *prarabdha* is, in a sense, a divine blessing, because it helps us to remember God. On such occasions, those who haven't prayed to God before even once begin to cry out to God. We see them turning to the path of *dharma*. By turning to

---

[13] The fruit of past actions from this and past lives, which will manifest in this life.

the spiritual path, they experience a lot of relief from the miseries of their *prarabdha*.

Most people are frightened when they hear of spirituality. Spirituality doesn't mean that you shouldn't acquire any wealth or that you should give up family life. You can become wealthy and lead a family life, but your life should be based on an understanding of the spiritual principles. Family life and the acquisition of wealth, without any awareness of the spiritual principles, is like collecting combs for a bald head! Our wealth and our relationship with our family are not going to be with us always. We should therefore accord them only the place they deserve in life.

It's not that we have to give up everything. The spiritual principles can teach us how to live wisely and happily in this material world. A person entering the sea without knowing how to swim could be swept away by the waves; it would be dangerous. But those who know how to swim enjoy swimming amidst the waves. For them, swimming is a joyful game. Similarly, by understanding spirituality, we can embrace the world even more joyfully. Spirituality is not simply the means to go to heaven, nor is it a bunch of superstitions. Heaven and hell are in this world itself. If we look at this world as a child's play, we can raise our minds to the plane of spiritual experience. Spirituality teaches us how to gain the courage and strength to enjoy bliss in this life itself. This path doesn't encourage us to sit idly by without doing any work. If a person who normally works eight hours a day extends it to ten hours and saves the extra income to help the suffering, that is true spirituality – that is real worship of God.

Chanting the Thousand Names

Some of Amma's children have come to Amma expressing their uneasiness. Someone told them that those who chant the *Lalita Sahasranama* (the Thousand Names of the Divine Mother) and worship the Divine Mother are thieves. Perhaps the person made this remark after seeing the excessive spending on pomp and luxury by others in the name of prayer. Or that person may have thought that chanting the Thousand Names is done to please some deity sitting somewhere high up in the sky. But we actually chant the Thousand Names to awaken the divine essence within ourselves, not to propitiate some divinity up above. God, who pervades everything, everywhere, resides also in our hearts. The *Sahasranama* is a way to awaken us to that divine level of awareness.

Each mantra of the *Lalita Sahasranama* has profound meanings. Take the first mantra: *Sri Matre Namah* – 'Salutations to the Mother.' The Mother is the personification of patience and forgiveness. When we chant this mantra, that *bhava* (divine mood, attitude or state) is awakened within us. We are asked to chant the mantra to nurture the quality of patience within us. Each of the Thousand Names is as important as the mantras in the *Upanishads*. When we chant the Names, we are unconsciously elevated to a more expansive state. The *Sahasranama* is meant to elevate us from the mentality (*samskara*) of a housefly to that of Divinity. That is true *satsang*.[14]

There were two boys in a family. The father took one of the boys with him wherever he went. When the father played cards with his friends, the boy sat next to him. He watched his father drink alcohol. The mother kept the other son with her. She told him inspiring stories and took him with her to the temple. In the end, the boy who grew up with the father developed a bad character. There was not a single bad trait he didn't have. On the other hand, the boy who grew up with the mother talked only about God and sang only divine songs. Love, compassion, and

---

[14] Being in the company of the holy, wise, and virtuous. Also a spiritual discourse by a sage or scholar.

true humility developed in that boy. As this example shows, our environment strongly influences our *samskara*. [15]

We awaken the divine *samskara* within us by chanting the *Sahasranama* and worshipping in a temple. When we meditate and chant a mantra with concentration, the divine power within us is awakened. It is good for the atmosphere as well. If one's will is one-pointed, anything is possible. But people today don't believe in such things. Sometime ago, when the spacecraft Skylab was about to fall back to earth, the scientists urged everyone to pray that it would fall into the ocean and not onto any inhabited area. They acknowledged that one-pointed prayer has great power. When the scientists said this, everyone began to believe it. The great sages revealed the power of the mind and the power of mantras long ago, but it is hard for us to accept this. We see scientists correcting their own earlier statements, yet as soon as they make a declaration, we are ready to accept it.

When we chant a mantra, we are attempting to awaken the Divinity within us. When we germinate beans, their nutritional quality and vitamin content increase. Chanting a mantra is a similar process that awakens our latent spiritual power. Moreover, the vibrations from the chanting purify the atmosphere. If we just close our eyes, we can see where our mind is. Even as we sit here, the mind dwells on all the things that need to be done when we get home. "What bus should I catch? Will it be crowded? Will I be able to go to work tomorrow? Will the money I lent so-and-so be returned to me?" A hundred thoughts like these dance through the mind. Turning a mind wrapped up in a hundred thoughts towards God cannot be done in an instant. It requires constant

---

[15] Samskara has two meanings: the totality of impressions imprinted on the mind by experiences from this or previous lives, which influence the life of a human being – his or her nature, actions, state of mind, etc.; the kindling of the right understanding (knowledge) within each person, leading to the refinement of his or her character.

effort. Chanting a mantra is an easy way to achieve this. Try to catch a child and he will run away. If we run after the child, he could fall into a nearby pond or well. But if we hold up a toy while we call out to him, he will come to us. In this way, we can avoid the possibility of the child's falling while running. Similarly, chanting a mantra is a way to make the mind do our bidding, taking advantage of its own nature. If a hundred thoughts arise in the mind, we can reduce them to ten by chanting a mantra. You may wonder if there won't be thoughts in your mind while you chant the mantra. Even if there are, they are not that important. Thoughts are like a baby: when the baby sleeps, it is easy for the mother to do the household chores; but once the baby wakes up and starts crying, it is difficult for her to work. Likewise, the thoughts that arise while we chant are not much of a problem; they won't bother us.

Some may wonder if a mantra isn't a thought. But isn't it true that the few letters contained on the poster saying "Stick No Bills!" help us to avoid a wall full of advertisements? Similarly, with the single thought represented by the mantra we can stop the mind from roaming. Reducing the number of thoughts is also good for our health and prolongs life.

The warranty period of an article begins only the instant we buy it, regardless of how many years the article has been lying in the store, because it hasn't been used. Similarly, a mind without thoughts doesn't weaken; it only gets stronger. The owner of such a mind becomes healthier and lives longer. On the other hand, when thoughts increase, the mind gets weaker and the person's health also suffers.

We know the stories of people in ancient times who performed penance, standing on one leg or even standing on a nail to keep the mind steady. There is no need for us to do anything like that. Just repeating a mantra is enough. Those people realized

God only after learning all the scriptures and spending ages performing austerities. But the *gopis*[16] never learned any scriptures. They were housewives and business women. Yet, their love for the Lord was so strong that they realized him easily. Especially in this *Kali Yuga*[17] (Dark Age), repeating a mantra is the most important thing.

However, chanting a mantra and doing spiritual practice is not enough. We can attain God only if we surrender our minds completely to Him. But the mind isn't something we can surrender as such. We can surrender the mind only by surrendering that which the mind is most attached to. Today wealth is what the mind is usually most strongly attached to. After they get married, people are often more concerned about their property than about their wives and children. Even when the elderly mother is on her deathbed, her son is making every effort to ensure that the share of the family property he will inherit contains more coconut trees than that of his other siblings. If he gets a little less than the others, he won't hesitate to stab his parents to death. So, what are we most attached to? To wealth! Since the mind is attached to wealth, to surrender one's wealth is to surrender the mind. God doesn't need our wealth. But through our surrender, our minds become expansive and we qualify for God's grace.

Service and spiritual life

Many people ask, "Why does Amma give so much importance to service? Aren't *tapas* (austerities) and spiritual practices more important?" My children, Amma never says that *tapas* and spiritual practice aren't necessary. Some form of *tapas* is necessary. If an ordinary person is like an electric post, a person who does

---

[16] Cowherd girls and milkmaids who lived in Vrindavan. They were Krishna's closest devotees and were known for their supreme devotion to the Lord.

[17] There are four yugas (ages or aeons). The world is currently going through the Kali Yuga.

tapas is like a large transformer that can be of service to many more people. The power to do this can be acquired through performing austerities. But it is not something you can begin doing when you are in your sixties with little health and vitality. *Tapas* has to be done when one is healthy and full of energy. There's no need to leave home and go to the Himalayas in order to do *tapas. Tapas* should be done right here in the midst of society. However, only those who dedicate the power they gain from their *tapas* for the benefit of the world can be called true spiritual beings. Spirituality asks you to be like an incense stick, giving fragrance to others while it burns itself out.

A person who gives up home and wealth, and sits in some cave somewhere doing *tapas*, is like a lake in a dense forest. Its water is of no use to anyone. And who benefits from the beauty and fragrance of the lotuses that blossom there?

It is true that long ago people used to go to the Himalayas to do *tapas.* But they went there only after selflessly leading the lives of householders. As householders, they matured and were mentally purified, and only then did they renounce all material wealth. The atmosphere in those days was conducive to doing *tapas.* People were aware of *dharma.* The rulers were truthful. Householders led their lives with Self-realization as their goal.

Nowadays people are selfish. Householders are just people with families; they are not *grihasthashramis.*[18] They don't even know what selfless service means. It is therefore important that spiritual people who have been enriched by doing *tapas* and spiritual practice live as models of selfless service for the world to follow. Only such individuals are really able to serve the world in a truly selfless manner.

---

[18] A grihasthashrami is someone who is dedicated to leading a spiritual life, while at the same time carrying out his or her responsibilities as a householder. It is considered to be the second of the four stages in life.

Selfless service is a spiritual practice that leads to Self-realization. Selfless service is true worship of God. When we discard our selfishness, the path to the Self opens up. Only when selfless seekers live as models for the world by performing selfless service, are people able to imbibe this principle. One has to go down to the level of the people to uplift them. We can move only in step with the times. Amma remembers a story related to this.

A *sannyasi* (monk) came to a village and the people made fun of him. He had some *siddhis* (miraculous powers), but he lacked forbearance. He got angry when the villagers ridiculed him. He took some ash, chanted some mantras, and threw the ash into the village well, with the curse that anyone who drank the water from that well would go crazy. There were two wells in that village, one for the villagers and the other for the use of the king and his minister. All the villagers went crazy after drinking the water from their well. The king and the minister drank the water from the other well and were unaffected. The villagers started blabbering and danced around and made a lot of noise. They were surprised when they noticed that the king and his minister weren't behaving like them. "Those two have changed a lot," said the villagers. In their eyes, the king and the minister were the crazy ones! Indeed, the villagers loudly declared that the king and his minister were now crazy. What do you do if those who are supposed to rule the land go completely crazy? The people decided to put the king and the minister in chains. A big commotion began. The king and the minister managed to escape and ran away. The crowd chased after them. As they ran, the king and his minister said to each other, "The people have gone mad. If we appear to be different from them, they won't spare us; they will accuse us of being crazy. If we are to survive and help them out of their situation there's only one thing we can do. We have to act as they do – because one has to act as a thief to catch a thief!" The king and the minister began to imitate the crowd and they danced and made strange noises. The people were pleased about this. They thanked God for curing the king and the minister of their madness.

My children, spiritual people are like the king and the minister in the story. In the eyes of ordinary people, spiritual people are crazy; but, in truth, it is those who have no interest in spirituality who are mentally deranged. Spiritual people have to go down to the level of worldly people to nurture good attitudes within them and to guide them along the right path. They may have to stay among the people and do many things. Only in this way can the people be guided towards the awareness of their true nature. People are not aware of their true nature. Are they themselves ready to search for their true nature?

Imagine, for example, that everything in a country suddenly shrinks to half its normal size. Things that were six hundred feet shrink to three hundred. People who were six feet tall become three feet tall. There is only one man who doesn't shrink. He remains six feet tall. But in the eyes of the others he is now deformed! Only he knows what has really happened. But who listens? The others are unaware that the six-feet-tall man is of normal height and that they are the ones who have become different.

My children, spirituality is the way to learn about our real nature. Spiritual people are aware of their real nature. They are attempting to realize their true Self. Others scorn them and call them crazy. Those people are deluded by the outer world. This is the difference between spiritual beings and others.

The devil of suspicion

Amma would also like to talk about the family problems that occur these days. Suspicion is the cause of most family fights. Many families have become separated because of mere suspicion. How many women have shed endless tears! Recently, a woman came here who had been abandoned by her husband because of his suspicions of her. She was about to commit suicide together with her three children. But then someone told her about the Mother in Vallickavu, and that she would get peace of mind if she went there. So she hurried here to Amma. Amma knows a lot of women like that. The husband doesn't contribute a penny towards household expenses, while the wife works day and night to take care of the home and children. What she gets in return for this is a sound beating at night when the husband comes home drunk. There are countless families like this around us, suffering and shedding tears. Sometimes the wife is thrown out of the house because of some suspicion on her husband's part. Where can she go at night with the children? Today, the situation in this land is such that it isn't safe for a woman to walk on the streets after dusk. Either her body will be found at the side of the road the next day or her future will be totally ruined. Conditions have deteriorated to this extent. Amma's male children who are present here shouldn't get upset. Amma is saying this for the sake of your daughters as well.

Parents give their daughter in marriage to someone working in the Persian Gulf. Anyone can write a false letter and the poor girl will be sent away. The next day she has to return to her parental home where she becomes like an orphan. She is at fault in the eyes of the neighbors, who don't know the truth. What will be the future of her child? My children, who thinks about these things? Just because people blindly believe someone's accusations, a whole family is destroyed. Thus a young woman ends up spending her life in tears.

Amma is thinking about starting an organization to aid the women who have lost all support in this way. For this, some very smart women with a lot of patience have to come forward and help. Then we can save thousands of families. Amma may end up being criticized for this. So be it. This doesn't worry Amma. She accepts it as the food of her life.

Amma remembers a story. Some things were stolen from a man's house. He had a close friend and started thinking, "It must be my friend who stole my things! He actually seems a bit nervous nowadays whenever he sees me. From the look on his face, anyone can see that he's a thief. And just look at the way he walks! All the signs of a thief are there. He is definitely the one who stole my things!" Thus, in his eyes, his closest friend became a first-class thief. He forgot how loving his friend had always been and saw him only as a thief and an enemy. However, all of this was just the creation of his own mind. That is what suspicion is like. Once you are afflicted with suspicion, you change completely.

Many couples who decide to break up their marriage due to mere suspicion would discover that there are no grounds for their suspicions, if only they were to talk to each other with open hearts. The problem would disappear like the peeling of an onion; there would be nothing left of it. By God's grace, Amma has been Instrumental in bringing countless such families back together, and in this way, the futures of many children have also become secure.

Give in charity instead of wasting your wealth

Amma can't help thinking about the recent earthquake. There's no use talking about it now. What is needed is to bring relief to those who are suffering over there. The Ashram Trust wants to donate four or five hundred thousand rupees. The devotees should come forward and give as much as they can to this cause. Charity is essential in the life of a householder.

Speaking on this subject, Amma remembers a story. A man decided to enter politics. But a friend told him, "Don't go into politics, because if you do you'll have to give away everything you have." "Fine, I will do that." "If you have two cars, you will have to donate one of them." "That's definitely no problem!" "If you have two houses, you'll have to give one of them away." "Sure, I'll do that too." "Also, if you have two cows, you'll have to give one of them to someone who doesn't have a cow." "Oh, no! That's impossible!" "Why not? You have no problem giving away your car or your house. Then why do you hesitate to give away just a cow?" "Because I don't have two cars or two houses. But I do have two cows!"

My dear children, this is the nature of people's generosity nowadays. They are more than willing to donate what they don't have, but unwilling to donate what they do have! My children, this is not what our generosity should be like. If we can help someone – even if we have to struggle a little to do so – this is the greatest way of worshipping God. The money we overspend on food and clothing would be enough to serve countless people. Think of how much money we are wasting now.

Nowadays many people think they're tough only if they smoke cigarettes, that smoking is a sign of masculinity. There are also those who think smoking is a sign of intelligence. Actually, it is a sign of mental retardation! True intellectuals are those who love others just as much as they love themselves. It is written on the cigarette package itself that smoking is hazardous to your health. If people smoke even after reading that, should they be called intellectual or idiotic? The money smokers spend in a month is enough to alleviate the poverty in India.

My children, today the world's population is a billion more than what it was fifteen years ago. In India, millions of children are born every year. If this continues, what will the situation be like ten years from now? As the population multiplies, the values in life are falling instead of rising. If we don't take each step carefully, the future will be dark. Therefore, there shouldn't be more than two children in each family. Those who don't have children should take the responsibility of raising some children from poor families who have many children. Try to impart a positive *samskara* in the children. We should be dedicated to living our lives in such a way that *dharma* is maintained. True spirituality is to dedicate one's life to the protection of *dharma*. My children, you should attempt to mold your minds for this purpose.

Amma is not going to trouble you with more words. My children, close your eyes and pray for world peace. Pray sincerely that you will be given the selfless heart of a mother. Shed a few tears at God's feet.

All of you, sit straight and meditate for two minutes. Imagine that you are seeing a bright light the size of a pinhead. Then visualize this light expanding in a circle and finally engulfing you completely. In your heart, call out like a small crying child, "Mother! Mother!"[19] Pray with your heart melting with love. Try to fill your heart with innocence. When a flower is still a bud, we cannot enjoy its beauty or fragrance. It has to blossom! Make your heart blossom! Then you can embrace God. Just as a child takes a pebble and imagines that it is the whole world, visualize the Divine Mother within you, and pray innocently. Forgetting everything else, cry out, "Mother! Mother!" – and pray to her with a melting heart, "Mother, make me do good deeds, make me compassionate, make me large-hearted!"

---

[19] Amma says that the Supreme Being is both our Father and Mother, God and Goddess, and is ultimately beyond any definition of gender.

This moment alone is real
Amma's birthday message 1994

Salutations to all the Children of Immortality, who are verily the embodiments of Love and the Supreme Self.

My children, all of you have come here today to celebrate Amma's birthday. But Amma can't see that there's anything special about this day that is not to be found on other days. The sky doesn't have any special day. The sky remains constant, as a witness of days and nights. Before this building was constructed, the sky was here, and it remains here since the building has been erected. The sky will be here after this building has been pulled down. The sky doesn't change. Everything exists within it, within space, and no one can pollute that space. By sky, Amma doesn't mean the sky we see above us, but the Self that is present everywhere and pervades everything.

If you ask why Amma came here today for the *pada puja* (the ceremonial washing of her feet), the answer is that Amma has come not for her own happiness, but only for yours. A birthday should be a day when we remember death as well as birth, because when we are born, death is born as well. We tend to forget this. Anyone who is born cannot possibly avoid death, for it follows everyone like a shadow. But many are afraid even to think about death.

Amma recalls a story. A brahmin once came to King Yudhisthira[20] asking for some money to meet the expenses for the marriage of his daughter. The king, who was very busy, asked the Brahmin to come back the next day. The king's brother, Bhima, who was standing nearby, heard this. He told everyone in the

---

[20] The eldest of the five Pandava brothers depicted in the Mahabharata. He was a king and renowned for his perfect virtue and piety.

palace, "Blow the conch! Beat the drums! Make joyous music with all your instruments! Cry out in joy!" The palace then resounded with all these different sounds. Yudhisthira was surprised. "What's all this?" he asked. "Normally, only when the king returns victorious from battle after conquering an enemy kingdom does such revelry take place. Nothing like that has happened now, so why all this commotion?" Those around him said, "Bhima asked us to do this!" At once, the king called for Bhima and asked him to explain.

"This is to show the joy that the people and I feel," said Bhima.

"What has brought so much joy?"

"You see, today I came to know that my brother has conquered death! So, that was in celebration of that victory."

Yudhisthira was puzzled. He looked at Bhima in dismay. Bhima said, "I heard you tell that Brahmin to come back and receive his gift tomorrow. But there is no guarantee that we will be here tomorrow. And yet, you were able to confidently tell the brahmin to be here tomorrow. Is it not true, then, that you said this because you have the ability to keep death away?"

Only then did Yudhisthira realize his mistake. He had forgotten the truth that death is ever present and that what needs to be done at this moment must be done now itself. Each time we breathe out, we cannot be sure that we will breathe in again. Death is with us during each breath.

Only someone who has understood what death is can build a true life, because at some point death will snatch away this body that we think is the real 'I,' and our wealth, children, and near and dear ones along with it. If we remember the truth that death is always with us, whether we are afraid of it or not, we can turn our life onto the right path and rise to a state that is beyond birth and death. Understanding what death is helps us to understand life. Everybody tries in vain to make their lives perfectly happy.

The reason for this failure is that whatever we gain today will be lost tomorrow, and those losses immerse us in unending sorrow. But when we become aware of the perishable nature of things, losing them will not weaken us – on the contrary, we will be inspired to rise to a state that transcends the loss of those things. We should begin this very moment to make every effort to achieve this state, because there is no assurance, whatsoever, that we will still be here a moment from now.

If this moment is lost, it is a great loss indeed. If you want to meditate, do it this instant. If there is a task that needs to be done now, it should be started at this very moment and not be postponed until a moment later. This is the state of mind we need to have. This sort of determination should take root in us. Whether we think of death or not, we are killing each cell in our body by thinking only of experiencing external happiness. The way of life we have adopted is poisoning us, and we are extending both our hands towards it and accepting it without realizing it is poison.

All countries, politicians, and scientists try to enhance the comforts of life. In order to do this, they have developed their intellects to the maximum extent. The external world has been developed as much as possible. But is there perfect happiness or contentment? No. The internal world continues to dry up. We may have air-conditioned homes, cars and planes, but isn't it true that we can sleep undisturbed only if we have peace of mind? And does a person who lacks inner peace eat healthily?

Live knowing the Truth

The quality of life does not depend only on the body, external objects, and external happiness. True happiness depends on the mind. If we can keep the mind under control, everything will be within our grasp. True knowledge is the knowledge of how to control the mind. This is spiritual knowledge. Only when we have acquired this knowledge can we properly use all the other knowledge we have gained. In the olden days, there were as many as 30 to 50 members in some families, and they lived together with such tremendous love, acceptance, and unity! There was an atmosphere of love and peace among them, and this was possible because they understood the spiritual principles. They understood life and its true purpose. They built their lives on the foundation of spirituality. But, today, all that is considered no more than a myth. Nowadays, if there are three members in a family, they live as if each one is on a separate island. Each individual has his or her own ways; there is no sense of unity. If we learn to understand spirituality, we can eliminate that situation, at least from our own family.

Spirituality is the principle that brings our hearts closer to each other. Those who have learned how to swim in the ocean will enjoy the waves. Each wave will delight the swimmers. On the other hand, those who don't know how to swim may get swept away by the force of the waves. Similarly, one who knows spirituality will face each obstacle in life with a smiling face.

Spirituality is the principle that allows us to face each situation and crisis in life with a smile. Those who aren't familiar with this principle will be shattered by even a minor obstacle. If a huge firecracker goes off when we are standing somewhere unaware, it will startle us; but if we know that it's about to go off, we won't be shocked. If we are aware, we won't falter when we are confronted by adverse circumstances.

Some people think spirituality is blind faith. But spirituality is the ideal that removes darkness. Many individuals mislead younger people instead of explaining the true spiritual principles to them. Some argue that, after all, religion isn't food for the hungry. This is true, but let Amma ask them something. Why do many people who eat sumptuously, sleep in air-conditioned rooms, and own yachts and airplanes kill themselves by taking poison, shooting themselves, throwing themselves under a speeding train, or hang themselves? Doesn't it point to the fact that there is something beyond the happiness that is gained from delicious food and luxuries? So what we need to accept and emulate in our lives is the peace-bestowing truth, and this is nothing other than the spiritual path. My children, to acquire houses and wealth, or to gain power and prestige, is like collecting combs for a bald head! This doesn't mean you should sit idly and do nothing. Perform every action without attachment after having understood this principle.

My children, all of us are different forms of the same Self, like the same candy in different wrappers. The candy in the green wrapper says to the candy in the red wrapper, "You and I are separate." The red one says to the blue one, "I am I and you are you; we are different." But if we remove the wrappers, they are all the same. The same sense of difference exists among us. Without realizing that in reality we are not different or separate from each other, we become deluded by the outer forms – and look at the problems that arise! Why don't people recognize this? Because we have lost the heart of the child within us. As a result, we don't know the essence of our true Self (*Atman*). We are unable to savor the bliss of Brahman.

When Amma talks about the heart of a child, she means a heart that can discriminate. You may say, "But children don't have any sense of discrimination." Actually, what is meant here is the faith and imagination of a child. A little boy takes a rock and calls it a decorated throne, and that is then what it becomes for him. When he stands in front of it, with a stick in his hand, and poses as a king holding a sword, in his mind he is indeed a king. His speech and his bearing will become those of a king. He doesn't think he is sitting on a rock or that he is holding only a stick in his hand. As far as he is concerned, he is wielding a real sword.

We have lost this power of imagination, faith, and innocence. Instead, we have become images of jealousy and ill will. A spiritual being needs an innocent heart and an intellect endowed with discrimination. Only then can one enjoy spiritual bliss. Sorrow or disappointment doesn't enter into the life of such a person.

My dear children, if you want to experience peace, you can't do this without an innocent heart. Only in an innocent heart can God reside.

A life full of uncertainty

Birds perch on tree twigs, where they eat and sleep. But they know that if the wind blows, the twig they are perching on could break. So they are constantly alert, ready to fly away at any moment. The things of this world are like such twigs; they may be lost at any moment. In order not to be overcome with grief when this happens, we have to hold fast to the Supreme Principle. If the house is on fire, none of us will say, "Lets put it out tomorrow!" We'll put out the fire immediately. Today our lives may be full of sorrow, but instead of brooding, ruining our health, and wasting time, we should try to find a solution.

My children, that which is with us now won't be with us forever. Our house, wealth, and property won't be with us always. In the end, none of these things will be our companions. Only the Supreme Being is our eternal companion. Amma isn't saying that we should give up everything or that we should feel aversion towards anyone. Amma means that we should recognize that nothing is permanent. We should live a life of detachment. This is the only way to find peace in life.

We are traveling by sea in a tiny canoe. Suddenly the sky darkens. There are signs of a storm: it begins to pour with rain and giant waves churn the sea. What do we do? Without wasting a moment we try to bring the boat ashore. My children, we are in a similar situation. We don't have even a second to waste. We need to row ahead towards the Supreme Being. This is our only refuge. Meditate constantly on the Supreme Being. This is the only way to eliminate sorrow.

My children, you are working hard for your own personal benefit, but don't forget to look around. Think of the torrential rain we've had in the recent months. There are thousands of people around us who have stayed awake under leaking roofs all through the rainy nights, wondering when their huts will collapse. When you raise your alcohol glasses, remember those people. With the money that we waste every month, we could get their roofs thatched. Then those people could sleep comfortably at night. There are so many poor children who, despite being the best students in their classes, have to stop going to school due to lack of money, and they become street children. Every time you dress in expensive clothes, imagine the faces of those innocent children.

My children, Amma isn't forcing anyone. She just remembers the plight of the world, that's all. There is one thing Amma is sure of: if her children are earnest, they can change the present conditions. My children, this alone would be true worship of God! This is what Amma expects from you.

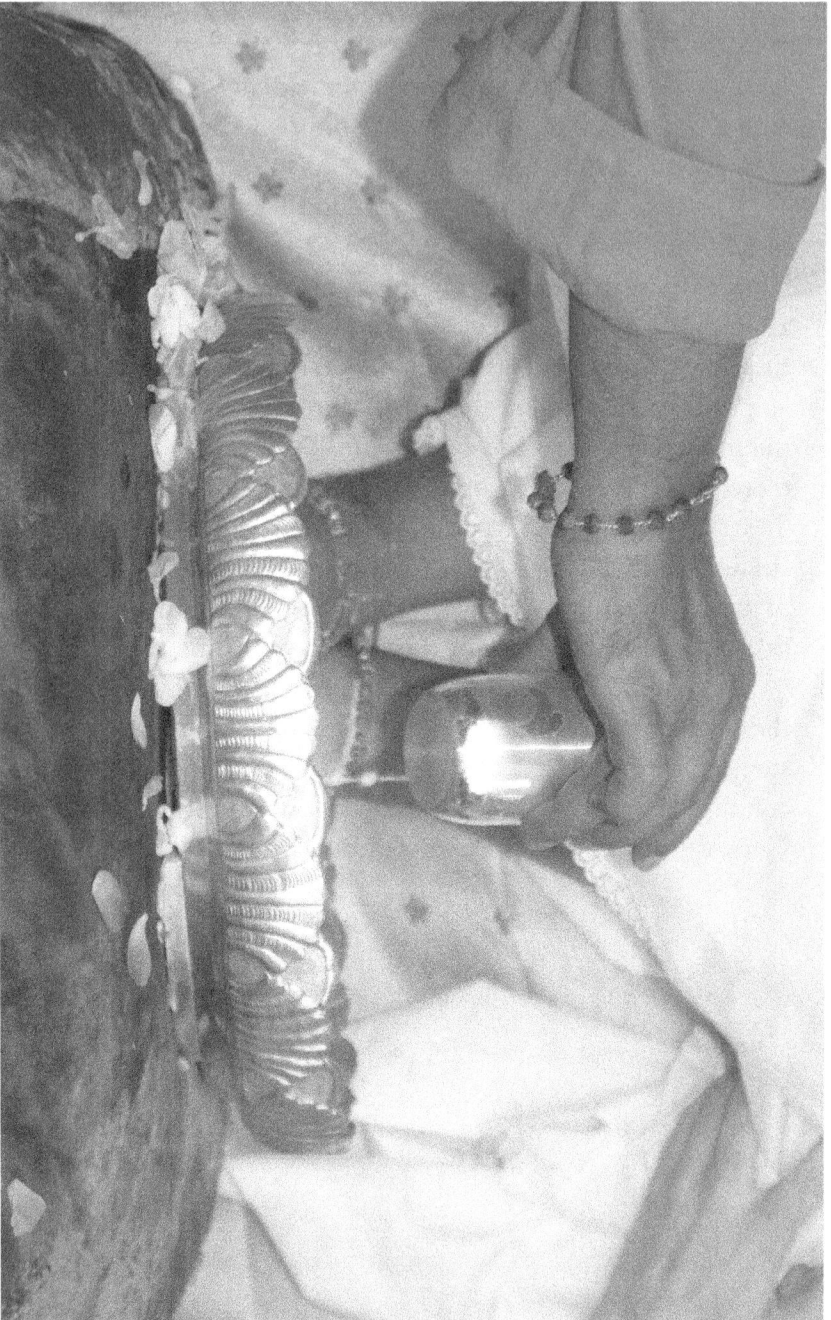

Swami Amritaswarupananda doing pada puja during Amma's birthday celebrations

I am Love, the embodiment of Love
Amma's birthday message 1995

My children, humility and patience are the foundation of everything. We need to have this attitude of mind. This attitude is absent now, and this is why conflicts arise in society. Today, the world has become a battlefield. In such a world there are no relatives, friends, or dear ones – only enemies eager to destroy one another. One moment they gang up and fight the opposite side; the next moment they split up and start fighting each other. This is what we see in many places. People have made it their business to be selfish and arrogant, and it isn't possible to know what their next move will be. So, my children, try to cultivate patience, love, and trust towards one another.

My children, we don't realize the truth that we are in bondage because of our attachment to our relationships. Not that we shouldn't have relationships, but when we develop attachments, we should clearly be aware of the place we give that object or person in our life. Only when the relationship is one of mutual understanding will true love develop. Whether the attachment is to a person or to an object, it shouldn't grow or weaken according to the circumstances. People say, "I love you!" – but those are not the right words. "I *am* love, the very embodiment of love" – this is the truth. When we say, "I love you," there is an "I" and a "you." And love gets squeezed somewhere in between. What flows from us to others should be love and nothing but love. Love shouldn't increase or decrease according to the circumstances. We should all learn to be the embodiments of love. Then, we will harm no one and will only benefit others. This is the principle we should realize.

Like a bird with clipped wings in a golden cage, we are imprisoned in our own minds. We are bound by the chains of name and fame, position and wealth, and those chains are covered with beautiful flowers. The question here is not one of freedom, but how to break the chains that bind us. In order to do this, we have to see the chains attached to us, and not the flowers. The flowers and decorations are only superficial. If we look more closely, we can see the chains that are hidden by the flowers. We need to see the prison as a prison, not our home. Only then will our minds leap eagerly towards freedom. Only then can we reach our goal.

Two plus two equals...

In the family life of today, the man will say that two plus two equals four, while for the woman, two plus two equals not only four – it could equal anything! The man lives in his intellect while the woman lives in her heart. Amma's women children need not be upset when they hear this. There is femininity in men and masculinity in women. Generally speaking, men's decisions are firm and do not yield to circumstances. From a man's earlier conduct, we can predict how he will act in every situation. But with a woman it is different; her nature is weaker, one that yields to circumstances. Her heart is one of compassion. This compassionate nature is the main cause of her sorrows. One cannot predict how a woman's mind will react to a given situation.

We go on our life journey with the heart and intellect. The heart and intellect are pointing in almost opposite directions. Because of this, there is often no peace or harmony in family life. Spirituality is the family member that brings together the diverging heart and mind into the proper rhythm and harmony. Spirituality is the link that connects them. Only when we give spirituality its due place does life become true life. The intellect doesn't ordinarily come down to the heart, and the heart doesn't rise to the intellect. This is how family life is proceeding now.

Many women complain to Amma and say, "Amma, I tell my husband all the sorrows of my heart. He just makes an acknowledging sound, but doesn't really respond at all. So I don't believe that he loves me." Amma then immediately asks the husband, "What is this I hear, son? Don't you love this daughter?" And he says, "It's not like that, Amma! I really love her!" My children, this is like honey inside a stone; one cannot taste its sweetness. To savor the sweetness, we have to get the honey out onto the palm of our hand. Similarly, love isn't something to be kept hidden inside; love should be shown at the proper times. The wife doesn't get happiness from the love that lies hidden in her husband's heart. My children, since you don't know each other's hearts, it's not enough to keep your love hidden inside your hearts. You have to *show* your love – with words and deeds. Amma is saying this for the sake of peace and harmony in family life. If you don't show your love, it is just like placing a block of ice in the hands of a person tormented by thirst. The ice cannot quench anyone's thirst. So, my children, you should go to each other's levels and love each other with open hearts. You should understand each other's love.

Amma remembers a story. In a certain family, the wife was very fond of animals. One day they went to a pet shop where the wife spotted a monkey and felt a great desire to buy it. But her husband refused to let her buy it. Later, when they returned home, her love for the monkey hadn't faded. One day when her husband was away, she went back to the pet shop and bought the animal. When her husband returned, he saw the monkey tied to a post. "What have you done?" he said. She replied, "I couldn't help it. I went and bought it!"

"But how will you feed it?"

"We'll give it some of our food."

"And where will it sleep?"

"On our bed."

"Oh, but it will stink awfully!"

"So what? If I could bear it for the last twenty years, I'm sure this poor animal can bear it as well!"

What does this mean? It means that in this worldly life, love is only skin deep. Today, people's love is rarely based on mutual understanding. Their hearts do not know each other. The wife doesn't understand her husband's heart, nor does the husband understand his wife's heart. No one is ready to compromise. This is how life proceeds. How can there be peace in such a life? Through spirituality we develop the readiness to understand and accommodate each other. The reason for all the failures in life is the lack of mutual give and take.

The first true love we experience is the love of our mother. You won't find any impurity in a mother's love for her baby. That love isn't based on any expectations whatsoever. Maternal love is essential for the growth of a baby. Even though the West is said to be the land of intellectuals, many people there are mentally ill. The reason for this is the lack of maternal love. Even if there is gasoline in the car, you need a battery to start the vehicle. Similarly, the love we get from the mother who gave birth to us is the foundation of our life.

You may ask, "But isn't the love shown by others also love?" Yes, that too is love – but there is always an expectation behind it. If the wife makes a mistake, her husband leaves her. If the husband makes a mistake, his wife leaves him. That sort of love is a love that vanishes when even a slight error is made. This is the nature of animal minds.

We love the cow for her milk, but when her milk dries up, we may keep her for a few more days and then sell her to the butcher. That is what worldly love is like. Amma cannot call that true love. Spirituality is what elevates that animal mentality to godliness. Husbands and wives may part company, but a mother isn't willing to give up her child; at least ninety percent of mothers are not. It is the mother's love that enables the child to accept love from the world and to give love. Remember this, my children: if a mother's love for her child disappears, that could be the cause of that child's downfall, as well as the cause of the downfall of the country.

Learn the language of the heart

This is a world of reason and intellect. People have forgotten the language of the heart. Today, the language of the heart, which loves, trusts, and respects others, has been lost.

A woman once showed her husband a poem she had written. She was a poet and her husband was a scientist. On the wife's insistence, he read the poem. It was a poem that described a child. "The child's face is like the moon, the eyes are like lotus petals…" – the poem contained similes like these on every line. When he had finished reading it, she waited eagerly for his opinion. He said, "What have you written here? Millions were spent for man to go to the moon, and what did they find there? Some rocks. Not even air. If you carry the moon on your head, your shoulders will be crushed!" He went on criticizing the poem with taunts like this. Finally she said, "You wouldn't understand this poem. Just give it back to me." The husband saw the poem through his intellect. There was no heart. He could only see the rocks on the moon. People have lost their innocence by insisting that they will trust only what they can see with their senses.

The intellects of people have grown so much that nowadays they cannot live without machines that do everything for them. There is even a machine that brushes one's teeth! Because of this, no one gets enough exercise. To maintain your health, you have to find time to exercise. When you consider this, you will see that the comforts gained in one way actually make us weaker in other ways. Today people are constantly feeling tense. All comforts and conveniences are available, but there is not even a moment free from tension.

Parents start worrying as soon as they find out that the baby, who is still in the womb, is a girl. Their worries don't end until they have brought her up, given her an education, and married her off. These days, they are just as worried about their sons. Even before the son reaches college, he wants a motorcycle, and there is no peace at home until he gets one. He won't hesitate to destroy anything he finds at home. He threatens to commit suicide if they don't buy him what he wants. These days, parents face many problems like this. Parents who hoped that their children would care for them when they grew up are now afraid of being killed by them! The progress of humanity has come to this stage. The reason is that today each individual is focused only on him- or herself. Selfishness has grown to this extent. As the intellect grows, the heart withers. The day is long gone when we felt that the sorrows of others were our own sorrows. Today people don't hesitate to place others in difficult circumstances for the sake of their own happiness. If this is to change, the heart has to expand along with the intellect.

Love should also flow down

Very often, we attempt to befriend people who are higher up on the social ladder or richer than we are. But that always causes sorrow. There are thousands who are going through greater struggles and misery than we are. Why don't we think about them? If we compare our lives with theirs, we can see that ours is heaven. When we think of those who are better off than we are, we grieve that we are so poor because we don't have the kind of riches they have. When we get sick we lament, "Oh no! I'm so sick!" But there are usually many people around us who are suffering from much worse illnesses than we are. If we were to think of them, our problems wouldn't seem so serious. We should try to gain freedom from sorrow by consoling our minds in this way. If we think the other way, our lives will be full of misery.

We are seldom willing to reach out to ordinary people. We don't find the time to share their sorrows. We are not ready to offer them whatever assistance we can. But, in fact, doing so is also a way of worshipping God. If only we were willing to do this, we would secure the key that opens the door to the world of joy.

Love the poor with an open heart. Empathize with them. Let us consider it our *dharma* to love them and to serve them. Let us see it as a duty entrusted to us by God. When we develop this attitude, we discover that we don't have time to grieve over our own plight. It is said that more than a third of India's population lives in poverty. If all of us are careful and eliminate unnecessary expenses, and help one another, no one will have to starve here. God has given us enough for everyone, but some have cornered for themselves what is meant for others. They don't know it is their own brothers and sisters who are suffering from starvation because of this. Such people may live in material pomp and splendor, but if they are not willing to be compassionate towards the poor and to help those in need, then they are suffering from inner poverty. In God's world they are indeed the poorest of the poor, and they won't be able to escape the mental suffering caused by their lack of compassion.

It is meaningless to light a sacred oil lamp or to make an offering to God without bringing some light into the lives of the poor. We have to go down to the world of the poor. We should love them and serve them. Without doing this, however much we meditate, we won't be able to taste the sweetness of that meditation. The help given to others is what imparts the sweetness to our meditation.

Amma sees people who are tormented because they cannot find work and have become slaves to drugs. Taking drugs won't give them jobs; it will only increase their family's burdens. Even if you have only ten cents[21] of land, try to grow something on it. Don't hesitate to practice some farming even if you've had a higher education. If nothing else is possible, at least grow a few banana plants in your yard. In this way, let us and our families live by our hard work.

My children, close your eyes now and visualize the form of the Divine Mother. Or imagine that the Divine Mother is standing in front of you. There is no need to think of inside or outside, or of the Supreme Being with or without attributes, etc. Just try to make your mind one-pointed. Don't worry if you cannot visualize the form. Close your eyes and call out quietly, "Mother! Mother!" Some people may ask, "But isn't God within us?" Yes, God is indeed within us, but we are not centered on our inner selves; our minds are running after many other objects. Repeating a mantra is a way of bringing the wandering mind inward. To say "Mother!" is the same as saying, "O Eternal Love! Eternal Compassion, lead me!"

Om shanti, shanti, shanti!

---

[21] One cent of land = 1/100 of an acre.

Reviving the ancient culture of the Rishis

Amma's birthday message 1996

Salutations to all of you, who are verily the embodiments of Love and the Supreme Self!

Spiritual beings don't have birthdays, anniversaries, and so on. They are supposed to give up all of that. Amma agreed to sit through all of this for the happiness of her children; however, the thing that would make Amma really happy would be if you were to make a vow on this day that you will imbibe the values of our culture, thereby reestablishing our *samskara*, and live according to that vow. We should make this firm resolve.

Many people raise the question, "Where are we heading?" This is a very important question. Where is India, the land of the *Rishis*[22] (the Self-realized sages of antiquity) heading? It is a question each one of us should ask ourselves. And it's almost too late. We cannot delay this any further, for delaying it would be dangerous. Amma isn't saying this to frighten her children. She is simply openly stating the truth. There is still room for hope. If we recognize the danger that lies ahead and proceed carefully, we can still avert it.

This is the age of untruth and unrighteousness. The society growing around us has lost its power of discrimination. Today, for whatever reason, the names of many of the individuals who should be guiding society have been tainted. The downfall of *dharma* is evident everywhere. It often occurs to Amma that we actually have to create a revolution. A *pralaya* (dissolution) has to take place here, and we shouldn't wait for the year 2000 for this to happen. The revolution has to happen here and now; we

---

[22] See Glossary.

cannot delay it for another minute. What Amma is referring to is a revolution of the mind. We have minds, but no conscience. We therefore need to purify our minds. Spirituality is an extraordinary gift that the ancient sages have given us. Without an understanding of spirituality, life would be filled with darkness. If we do not imbibe our spiritual culture properly, our lives will be meaningless.

On the other hand, if we understand spirituality and live in accordance with its principles, our lives will be full of meaning, beauty, and joy. It is therefore essential, from all perspectives, that we revive spirituality in our lives. Our Mother Dharma is afflicted with a heart disease. We urgently need to operate on her so that she will be cured. My children, today itself you should take a vow to do this.

Bharat, the land of dharma

Nowadays people are reluctant even to utter the word *dharma*. Bharat (India) is the land of *dharma*. *Dharma* is the principle of expansiveness, the essence of love. The *dharma* of India is said to be like the footprint of an elephant, which is so large it can contain the footprints of all other animals. Likewise, the *dharma* of India, the culture of India, is broad enough to encompass everything. But today it is perishing in every way. This must continue no longer.

Science and culture

Our culture is not something that arises out of science; it originates from *samskara*, and that *samskara*, in turn, has its origin in spirituality. Amma is not denigrating science – science gives us physical comforts and conveniences – but for *samskara* to be formed in life, spirituality is essential.

Where did this *samskara* of ours come from? We got it from the *Rishis*, the ancient sages. Our *samskara* carries within it the principles of life that belonged to the lineage of the *Rishis*. It is still within us; it hasn't perished completely. Today it has become essential that we revive and reestablish it.

We know what the sages did. The snow in the Himalayas melts in the heat of the sun and flows down in the form of numerous rivers for the benefit of the world. In the same way, the love, compassion, and grace of the sages, who are knowers of *Brahman*, the Absolute Reality, flow out to all living beings. Their love removes the ego in us, makes our minds as expansive as the universe, and inspires us to dedicate our lives to the good of the world. This is the *dharma* followed by the lineage of the *Rishis*. The uncontrolled lives of people today erect a wall that halts the flow of that love and selflessness.

The Guru and the disciple

The spiritual masters and the disciples of the ancient guru-kulas used to chant a certain mantra[23] together. The spiritual master was more exalted than the disciples sitting on the ground before him or her. Yet the master chanted this mantra together with the disciples.

Om sahanavavatu
Sahanau bhunaktu
Sahaviryam karavavahai
Tejasvinavadhitamastu
Ma vidvishavahai
Om shanti shanti shanti.

May God protect us all.
May He cause us to enjoy the bliss of the Self.
May we become valorous and magnificent.
May we strive together and may our studies be fruitful.

---

[23] This mantra is the introductory mantra (the Shanti Mantra or Peace Invocation) In all the Upanishads belonging to the Krishna Yajurveda. The Krishna Yajurveda is part of the Yajurveda, which is one of the four Vedas.

May we never quarrel with one another.
Om peace, peace, peace.

The lineage of the *Rishis* demonstrated this kind of humility. They didn't feel that their wisdom should benefit only themselves. Where is that wisdom which fostered humility and *samskara* now? What do we see in the schools today? The students think they are smarter than the teachers. The teachers react by thinking, "How arrogant they are! What can I teach them?" However, neither teachers nor students are ready to try to look into and understand this problem. As a result, the teachers have become mere machines and the students are like stone walls. There is no love between them, and no flow of knowledge is taking place. There was a time when the atmosphere in schools was very different. Both the teachers and children were full of eagerness. The children were eager to listen to the teacher, and the teacher was eager to impart his or her knowledge to the students. They were never bored, no matter how much time they spent together.

In olden days, the habit of taking notes and learning from notes was unknown in schools. Without the help of a pen or a book the students learned more than the people of today will learn in a lifetime. They committed the Vedas, the Vedangas,[24] Ithihasas,[25] and the epics to memory. Education, in those days, was what the disciples absorbed from the masters through love, and from sitting face to face with them. The disciples didn't know what fatigue was. They were developing at every moment.

Where there is love, nothing can ever be a burden. Like a blossoming flower bud, the disciple's heart is opened by the master's love. The master's grace flows spontaneously into the disciple's heart. The disciples back then were not just hearing each word

---

[24] Vedangas are branches of knowledge that are auxiliary to the Vedas.
[25] Epic history.

of the teacher; they were experiencing it. This was the mode of education in those days. What has happened to our educational system today?

Loving our children

In olden days, children were sent to school at the age of five. Nowadays children are often initiated into the alphabet when they are barely two and a half. They are brought here to Amma for this initiation as well.

Until children are five years old, they should just be loved and given freedom. Their freedom shouldn't be restricted. They should be allowed to play freely. We should make sure they don't hurt themselves – for example, that they don't burn themselves or fall into water – that's all. No matter what mischief they do, little children should only be loved. They should be brought up in the womb of love, just as they were carried in the womb of their mother. But this is not the situation today. Many of them are sent to school when they are too young, and they experience nothing but tension. It is like introducing worms into buds that are meant to blossom into beautiful, fragrant flowers! Even if the worm-infested buds blossom, they'll be misshapen. As children grow, their minds become stunted because of the unnecessary loads they are forced to carry. If this is to change, the parents first have to gain some understanding of spirituality, and then they should impart this to their children. Everyone should know the role of spirituality in life. Material education will help us get a job so that we can fill our stomachs, but life isn't fulfilled by that alone.

Spirituality – the fullness of life

Life becomes perfect only when we absorb spirituality. The absence of spirituality is the cause of today's problems. Without spirituality, we cannot eliminate the unrest in the world.

Recently, a very famous film actress committed suicide. She apparently had no one who loved her. When you don't receive any love from the person you expect it from, there is no sense of life left. That is what it is like in today's world. But this will not happen if one absorbs the spiritual principles. This understanding will teach us what true life and love are all about. Today, no one tries to revive or follow the *dharma* that leads to immortality instead of pushing them towards death. Instead, people shed tears, lamenting that life brings only sorrow. They commit suicide or dismiss *dharma* as being too old-fashioned. Instead of saying this, let us try to live according to *dharma*. Then we will realize what life truly is about, what happiness and beauty really mean.

Air-conditioning the mind

My children, while science air-conditions the outer world, spirituality air-conditions the inner world. Spirituality is the knowledge that air-conditions the mind. Spirituality has nothing to do with blind faith; it is the principle that dispels darkness.

If you hold chocolates in one hand and a gold coin in the other, and show them to a child, which hand will the child choose? The one with the chocolate. The child doesn't understand that you can buy many chocolates with that one gold coin. This is what we are like today. Due to the attraction of the material world, we lose our sense of reality.

God is the sweetness we can never feel satiated with. God is the source of both liberation and worldly prosperity. Today people are forsaking God and running after material gains that last only for a few moments. The result can only be disappointment. Each moment that you take refuge in God is bliss and prosperity. Nothing can equal that. The time spent meditating on God is never a waste. No one meditating on God has ever died of starvation. So one should never think that such meditation is a loss. We have to resurrect this path. We need to encourage others to follow this path. This can never be a losing business; you reap only profit from it.

God is experience

Only through meditation can we reach God who is within us. You cannot tell how beautiful or fragrant a flower is when it is still a bud. It has to blossom. My children, open the buds of your hearts! You will definitely be able to enjoy that bliss. We cannot see an electric current, but we can experience it if we touch a wire carrying electricity. God is an *experience*. Meditation is the way to that experience. Strive for that, my children, and you will certainly succeed.

Why?

Many children come to Amma saying, "Amma, I can't really laugh. I can't talk to anyone with an open heart. Amma, I'm always sad."

My children, ask yourselves the reason for that sadness. Ask yourselves, "What am I lacking that causes this sadness? What burden am I carrying?" If you do, you will find an answer.

Look at Nature. Look at that tree over there, how blissfully it sways in the wind. And look at those birds. They're singing, forgetting everything else. And that stream over there – how merrily it flows, singing melodiously. And those plants – and the stars, the sun, and the moon. Everywhere there is only joy. Being in the midst of all of that joy, why are we the only ones who grieve? Why are only we unhappy? Contemplate this and you will understand. None of those elements of nature has an ego. Only we do. "I am this and that, I want to become that, I want that" – this is what we think about all the time. But this 'I' we are so preoccupied with will not accompany us when we die. There is no benefit to be had from the sense of 'I.' If we hold fast to that 'I,' there will be nothing but suffering. So, my children, give up that 'I' and arise! Then you will be happy and rejoice. Be happy, my children. Only this moment is ours. We cannot be certain that we will take the next breath. So, try to rejoice, without grieving even for a moment. But this isn't possible without giving up the sense of 'I.'

This is a benevolent gift that the ancient *Rishis*, through their grace, have given us. My children, begin to live in accordance with this knowledge, without wasting even a moment. Otherwise, this life will be meaningless. Don't think you can do this tomorrow, because tomorrow is truly only a dream. Even now we live in a dream – that's all it is. While an ordinary dream ends in one night, this dream is a long one. Only by waking up from this dream can we know what reality is. And it is to God that we awaken. We should feel assured of this, for only then can we awaken from this dream. Each passing moment is extremely valuable, and shouldn't be wasted. It is foolishness to postpone our awakening until tomorrow and sink back into the dream. Tomorrow is a question without an answer. It is like adding four and four and saying it totals nine; it will never be nine. Nothing is more valuable than this moment that we have now. Don't ever let it go to waste. My children, grasp the present moment and learn to laugh with an open heart. Try to make sure that the smile on your lips never fades. Try not to harm anyone in thought, word, or deed.

Make this a moment of bliss

Today our minds dwell on the past and what is yet to come. Because of this, we lose the present moment, which is to be enjoyed.

A man bought some ice cream and placed it in front of him, ready to eat. He put a spoonful into his mouth and began thinking, "I have a slight headache. It started this morning. The restaurant where I ate last night wasn't clean; all the food was kept out in the open. Could a lizard or something have fallen into the food? That jewelry shop next to the restaurant – there were so many beautiful things on display there! And the clothes in the shop window across the street were so fashionable! Will I ever be able to afford such things? I can hardly survive on my present salary. What a life this has turned out to be! Oh, if only I had been born into a rich family! If only I had studied more at school! But it just didn't happen!" He kept thinking like this while eating the ice cream. He wasn't even aware of what the ice cream tasted like. His mind was elsewhere. During those moments he was as good as dead. Brooding about the past and what is yet to come, he wasted the wonderful moments he had been given to enjoy. That is why Amma says that the past is like a canceled check. It is useless to think about the past. Brooding over the past is like hugging a corpse! The people who are dead will never come back to us. The time that has gone by will not return. Similarly, it is useless to think about what may happen in the future, for that, too, is just a dream. It may or may not happen. Only this moment is useful.

It is like the money we have on hand. We can use it in any way we like, but if we spend it carelessly we won't get any benefit from it; the money will be lost. So, we should spend it thoughtfully. We should exercise discrimination at each step. Only then can we advance courageously on our path of action. We should be firm in our resolve to assimilate this principle.

The need for selfless action

Generally speaking, two things happen in life: we perform actions and we enjoy their fruits. If we perform positive actions, the fruits will be good, while only bad fruits can come from negative actions. Each action should therefore be done with great care.

Some people try to discourage those who perform actions. They have read books on Vedanta and say, "Isn't there only one Self (*Atman*)? Then, what other Self could this Self possibly serve?" But we can see that even those who ask this question are very attached to their physical needs. They eagerly await one o'clock so that they can have their lunch. They feel uneasy and get angry if they don't get their food exactly on time. Where does their knowledge of the Self go when they get hungry? They don't ask, "What is the need for food for the Self?" They don't compromise when it comes to bodily needs like eating, sleeping, wearing good clothes, and so on. They are reluctant only when it comes to doing good for others. This is not the true Vedantic view; it is merely the line of argument of lazy people who sit around doing nothing. It isn't of any use to us. True knowledge lies not in action as such, but in the actionlessness in feeling that one is truly not doing anything even while performing actions.

The truth is that not even for a moment can we not be doing something. If we are not active physically, we are active mentally. While asleep, we perform actions in our dreams. And our breathing and other bodily functions continue automatically. There is no way to avoid action. So, then, why not do something that will benefit the world in some way? And would it be wrong if this should happen to be physical work? Selfless actions weaken our innate undesirable tendencies. Only if our thoughts, words, and deeds are good can we overcome the tendencies we have accumulated so far.

In olden days, the spiritual masters gave tasks, such as gathering firewood, watering plants, and washing clothes, to the disciples who came to them to study Vedanta. Selfless service is essential for transcending selfishness and attachment to the physical body. So, no one should be idle or discourage those who work.

Those in whose hearts compassion springs up at the sight of the suffering of others cannot just sit and do nothing. God's grace will flow only to the heart that has such compassion. If divine grace happens to reach a place where there is no compassion, it will be of no benefit. It is like pouring milk into an unwashed pot. Inner purity can be achieved only by performing actions that benefit others.

There was once a king who had two sons. The time had come for the king to go to the forest and lead the life of a hermit.[26] Which one of his sons was to be his successor? He felt that the one who was to be king had to love the people. He was having a difficult time deciding. He brought his sons to his spiritual master, who could see into the future, and he explained his wish to the master. The master listened and said, "A few days from now I am going to an island nearby. Send the princes there. They shouldn't ride any horses or use any transportation. Don't send any servants with them either. Just give them some food for the journey."

On the day indicated by the master, the king sent the two princes to the island. As the master had instructed, he sent them without any transportation or entourage. The oldest prince set out first. On the way a beggar came up to him and pleaded, "I am starving to death! I haven't eaten anything for two days. Pray, give me something to eat!" The prince didn't like this at all. He scolded the people who were present. "Am I not the oldest son of the king? Is it right to let beggars accost me?" He warned that this must not happen again and continued on his journey.

Shortly afterwards, the younger prince came walking the same way. The same beggar went up to him and begged for food. The prince thought, "I ate this morning. This poor man says he hasn't eaten anything for two days! How terribly sad!" The younger prince continued on his way only after consoling the poor man and giving him the food parcel he was carrying.

To reach the island, the princes had to cross a river. When they reached the river bank they came across a leper, whose entire body was covered with pus-filled wounds. The leper couldn't

---

[26] Vanaprastha – the third stage of life.

swim. He was calling out for help to cross the river. The oldest prince held his nose against the stench of the leper and waded through the river.

However, the second prince felt he couldn't leave the poor leper stranded. "Poor man!" he thought. "If I don't help him, who will?" He lifted the leper onto his shoulders and waded into the river. Suddenly the water began to rise. A big landslide upstream had created a very powerful current in the river. The older prince couldn't get a firm foothold. The water rose rapidly. He tried to swim but failed, and was swept away by the current. Even though the water level kept rising, the younger prince wouldn't let go of the leper. He tried to swim while carrying the leper. His arms and legs grew weak. He couldn't hold on any longer. Just then he saw an uprooted tree floating down the river. He caught hold of it and made the leper do the same. Holding onto the tree, they safely reached the other bank. The prince then left the leper there and went to see the spiritual master.

It was the younger prince's compassion that returned to him as grace in the form of the tree that saved him. Grace comes automatically to those who are compassionate. One cannot escape from a very powerful current, no matter how good a swimmer one may be. Only divine grace is one's refuge then; and you cannot be given that grace without performing good actions. My children, each of our actions should be filled with compassion.

Grace is a must for success

We often see ads in the papers announcing job vacancies. The candidate must, for example, have a master's degree, be of a certain height, and produce a health certificate from a doctor, as well as a character reference. Only those who can meet those requirements can apply. When the written examination and the interview are over, it turns out that some of the people who answered all the questions correctly have not been selected for the job, while some of those who didn't do well at all on the questions have been selected.

This is a common occurrence. What is the reason? Those who were not selected didn't have the grace that would melt the heart of the interviewer, while those who had that grace got the job even though some of their answers were wrong. Thus, success in any effort also depends on grace. In any undertaking, only if that grace is present, over and above all human effort, will perfection be achieved. Only then can life flow forward. But that grace cannot be gained without purity in one's actions.

Giving only to the deserving

Ninety percent of Amma's children gathered here today haven't understood spirituality properly. Each person can assimilate things only according to his or her power of thinking and *samskara*. It is therefore necessary to go to each person's level when explaining things. We cannot give the same advice to everyone. The same words will be understood differently by different people. This is the reason for saying that one should know the listener before imparting spiritual instructions.

Suppose the shoes in a shoe shop are all the same style and size. Even if a hundred buyers come in, there is just one size available. That shop won't be of much use, even if it stocks plenty of shoes. Different sizes have to be available so that people can choose the size that fits them. Our culture, Sanatana Dharma[27] (the Eternal Principle) accommodates the many different paths. For people who come from diverse cultural backgrounds to be uplifted, each of them needs to be led along a path that is appropriate for his or her particular mind and circumstances in life. Only then can we take them to the goal.

---

[27] Sanatana Dharma is the traditional name of Hinduism.

There is one Truth – the sages call it by different names

Hinduism refers to many different deities. The rituals and observances prevalent in different parts of India differ. The people of India have grown up in different cultures. This land has been ruled by rulers from different countries. Because of this, different modes of worship suitable for the different cultures and deities came into being. But the Consciousness-Power that exists in all of them is one and the same. Whether you use green, blue, or red soap the lather will be white. Likewise, the Consciousness-Power of the different deities is the same. It is this Consciousness-Power, this one God, that we should realize. It exists within us as well. It is all-pervading. It is present in the singing cuckoo bird, the cawing crow, the roaring lion, and the thundering ocean. It is that same power that sees through our eyes, hears through our ears, tastes through our tongue, smells through our nose, feels through our skin, and powers our legs as we walk. It is this power that fills everything. It must be experienced.

Cultivate the attitude of surrender

Our devotion shouldn't resemble the condition of a baby monkey. The baby monkey clings to its mother's belly. As the mother jumps from one tree branch to another, the baby will fall to the ground if it loosens its clasp. Our prayer should be, "Mother, hold me!" We should have that sense of surrender. Then there is no need to fear. Even if our grip loosens, the firm hold of the Supreme will protect us.

The kitten knows only how to cry. Its mother will pick it up with her mouth and carry it to a place of safety. The kitten doesn't have to be afraid because its mother won't let go of it. We should pray, "O Mother, hold my hand and guide me!" As long as she guides us, we cannot fall into a hole or a ditch. She won't allow us to get lost among our toys (worldly attractions). She will guide us to the goal. This is the attitude we need to develop.

The practice of repeating a mantra

Repeating a mantra is a spiritual practice we can perform easily and always. My children, you came here by bus. Can you not chant your mantra from the moment you climb onto the bus until you reach here? And also on your way back? Why don't we make it a practice to chant while traveling? Why ruin our mental peace and health talking about other things during that time? By repeating a mantra, one gets not only mental peace but also material benefit. We gain not only God, but God's glories as well.

Service to humanity is service to Amma

As a result of the efforts that all of Amma's children have made, our ashram has had the good fortune of being able to render a great deal of service within a short span of time. If you put your minds to it, we can do so much more for the world. As soon as it became known that we were planning to build 25,000 houses for the poor, we got more than 100,000 applications from people wanting homes! Most of the applicants deserve to be given a house. If Amma's children decide to help, we can build a house for every person who doesn't have a place to sleep. There's no doubt about that. The money you overspend in your day-to-day lives would be enough to achieve this.

"From today onwards, I will not smoke. I will stop drinking alcohol. Instead of buying ten sets of clothes each year, I will buy nine." My children, make decisions of this kind, and use the extra money to build homes for the poor instead. Then, ten years from now there won't be any slum areas anywhere in the country. Some mothers come to Amma and say, "Amma, it was raining last night and our hut was leaking everywhere. To keep the baby from getting soaked, I had to hold a mat [made of woven straw or plastic] over her head." Imagine that, my children – the mother staying awake all night because of the pouring rain, holding a mat over her baby so that the baby could sleep without getting drenched inside the leaking hut! At the same time, there are people who spend thousands on alcohol and drugs.

Why did Amma decide to build so many houses? Because she was thinking about the suffering of her children. She didn't think about anything else. If we could do all of the other things we have done in such a short time, this is also possible. We have received 100,000 applications. We can build 5,000 houses a year. If all of you will it, we can build even more. Doesn't Amma have countless children? If you give up smoking for two years, we can build one house with the money that you save. Just two rooms are enough for a family to sleep in without being bothered by the rain. My children, remember this when you spend money unnecessarily.

Some of you use alcohol, *ganja* (hashish), and so on. My dear children, if you do that, you are really consuming blood and tears, the blood and tears of the mothers, wives,[28] children, and siblings in your family! My children, pray to God for the strength to eliminate such bad habits! Amma's food is the minds of her children that are free of jealousy and spite. If you have that sort of mind, then that is Amma's joy. So, pray to God, my children, to be free of all jealousy, and to gain the strength to do positive things! Pray for the strength to get rid of your bad habits. Pray for a mind that sees only the good in everything, like a honey bee that savors only the honey in every flower.

Amma always talks about surrender. Whatever you do, try to do it as an offering to God. Pray that you may see everything as God's will. Such surrender should be the aim of our lives.

---

[28] In Kerala it is very unusual for an Indian woman to smoke or take drugs.

An ideal for a free India

Amma's birthday message 1997

Salutations to all of you, who are verily the embodiments of love and the Supreme Self! All of my children have assembled here with patience and enthusiasm. If you can sustain these qualities throughout life, everything will come to you – because patience and enthusiasm are what give you success in life.

Some people are enthusiastic but have no patience. Others are patient but have no enthusiasm. Ninety percent of young people are enthusiastic, but we don't see much patience in them. They are hasty and do things at the spur of the moment. Because of their lack of patience, they often fail to achieve their goals. On the other hand, people in their sixties and seventies are often very patient. From their experiences in life they have acquired such qualities as patience, a sense of discrimination, and intelligence, but they don't have much enthusiasm. If you ask them why this is, they will say, "My body has lost its strength; I can no longer move the way I'd like to." This is what we see these days.

Look at a small child. She is both enthusiastic and patient. She tries to stand up, falls down, and tries again. She refuses to give up, even if she hurts herself in the process. Finally, she manages to stand up as a result of her continuous effort and because of the fact that she didn't lose her patience or enthusiasm. The child knows that her mother is there to protect her, to wipe the blood away and put ointment on a wound if needed. The toddler is optimistic about succeeding because her mother is nearby, always on hand to help the child in her efforts. Patience, enthusiasm, and optimism – these three qualities should be the mantras of our lives. In every field we can observe that those who have faith succeed while those who lack faith lose their strength.

A shoe company sent two men to sell its products in a distant village. Within a few days one of the salesmen sent a message back to the company: "The people here are all aborigines. They don't know anything about shoes. It would be impossible to sell anything out here, so I'm coming back right away." But the other salesman's message was quite different. He wrote: "The people here are aborigines. They don't know anything about shoes. They walk and sleep in the dirt. If we teach them about the benefits of wearing shoes, we can sell them a lot of sandals. So send a load of sandals right away!" The salesman with the optimistic faith succeeded.

If we have the faith that God is always with us to aid us in any crisis, we will get the energy and enthusiasm we need to transcend any obstacle in life, and our optimism to succeed will never leave us.

Rama, Krishna, Christ, and Mohammed all faced many obstacles, but they never faltered. They never looked back. They just kept going forward. As a result, success was always with them. They continue to live on, even today. When Amma says this, you may think, "But weren't they all *avatars*?[29] They could do those things, but how can ordinary people like us be anything like them?" My children, none of you is an ordinary person! Each of you possesses extraordinary powers. There is infinite strength within us, but it's sleeping at the moment. We just have to awaken it. Then, victory is certain.

Receiving grace

Our bodies have grown, but our minds haven't grown. For our minds to grow as large as the universe, we have to become like children. We have to awaken the child within us. Only a child can grow. What we have within us today is the ego, and

---

[29] Incarnations of the Supreme Being.

nothing can be gained with that sense of 'I.' It has to disappear, and a sense of expansiveness has to take its place.

To love God is to feel reverence towards everything; it doesn't just mean that we pray. God isn't someone sitting somewhere above the sky. God's abode is within each of us, and we need to develop this awareness. The main ingredient needed for this is humility. We have to learn to always have the attitude of a beginner, because then there is no arrogance. But in order to do this, we have to renounce something big. We have to renounce the 'I.' The sense of 'I' is the obstacle to everything. By letting go of it, we ensure success in our lives. It is said that for every success, God's grace is more important than the effort we make. Our ego is the obstacle to that grace. So, we somehow have to renounce the ego. Our renunciation will make us great.

However, to qualify for grace we need to create good *karma*. We always say, "Give me this! Give me that!" But we haven't learned to say "Thank you!" We have to learn to express gratitude in all circumstances. Instead of thinking of what we can get from others, we should always think about what we can do for others. This is the attitude we should cultivate.

A man went to visit a friend in his new house. When he arrived he stood outside for a while enjoying the beauty of the great mansion. When the owner came out to greet him, he asked in amazement, "How many people live in this house?"

"I live here alone," his friend replied.

"You live here by yourself! Is this your house?"

"Yes."

"Where did you get the money to build such a house at such a young age?"

"My older brother had this built for me. He has a lot of money."

As the visitor fell silent, his friend said, "I know what you're thinking. Don't you wish that you too had a brother like that?"

"No," said the visitor, "I was thinking that if only I were rich like your brother. Then, I, too, could have given away a house like that!"

My children, this is the attitude we should have, the attitude of wanting to give. Only those who give can receive. By giving we receive peace of mind.

Many types of waves travel in the atmosphere around us. Thoughts are also waves. This is why we say that each thought and word should be expressed with care. It is said that the tortoise hatches its eggs with its thoughts, the fish with its gaze, and the hen through body contact. Our thought waves are also powerful. If we get angry at someone who has not done anything wrong, he or she will feel hurt and say, "O God, I don't know anything about it! Why are they saying all this?" The wave of sorrow coming from that person will reach us and be captured by the subtle aura surrounding us, and the aura will absorb it. It will darken our aura like smoke covering a mirror. Just as smoke hinders light from falling on a mirror, the darkness caused by that wave of sorrow will prevent us from receiving divine grace. This is why we are asked to give up bad thoughts and to cultivate thoughts about God. By cultivating a constant remembrance of God, we become like God.

Some people think, "I'll become good when the others become good." This is like planning to bathe in the ocean after all the waves have subsided. We shouldn't waste any opportunity to do good for others, to help others. Any thought about people not having reciprocated should never keep us from doing good for others.

We have to cultivate compassion within us. Compassion should shine through each of our thoughts and words.

Actions and their fruits

It is sometimes said that our lives should be like our eyes, because our eyes will adjust their focus, depending on whether an object is near or far. This is how we are able to see things. Similarly, we should develop a mind that can adjust itself to any situation in life. This becomes possible through spirituality. We need peace in our hearts so that we can adjust to different situations. Only through meditation can we find true peace.

At present we are like obedient machines. This is not how we should be. We need to be awake and have a sense of discrimination. If ordinary life is like driving a car on the road, spiritual life is like flying a plane. The cars on the road can move only on the ground; they cannot rise even a little bit above the ground. But airplanes are different, for they move on the ground and then soar to great heights. When we rise to great heights, we gain the power to view everything as a witness.

Many people say they haven't knowingly done anything wrong and yet they have to undergo suffering. One thing is certain: we experience only the fruits of what we have done. We can never avoid this. If a calf is set free in the middle of a thousand cows, it will find its mother and go to her. Likewise, the fruits of our actions will come to us, and to us alone. God hasn't created anyone just so he or she may be punished.

There were three sons in a family. Their parents died. The boys were all college graduates, but hadn't found jobs yet. A wealthy man took pity on them. He invited them to his home and gave them jobs. All three of them were given the same position. One of them started taking bribes. The boss warned him several times, but he wouldn't listen. So, because he wasn't fit for a high position, he was removed from that position, and was given the job of a porter. The second brother was disciplined and honest. But he went to collect his pay exactly at the end of each month; he wouldn't wait for even one day beyond that. Because he was disciplined and truthful, the boss promoted him. The third brother was not like the other two. Like the second brother, he performed the job entrusted to him with honesty and discipline. However, he declined the salary offered to him at the end of each month, saying, "You gave me this job and a home. You provide me with food, clothes, and everything else I need – so why would I need a salary?" Some time later the rich man passed away. In his will, he bequeathed all his wealth to the young man who worked without accepting a salary. In the end, the person who worked honestly was elevated to a higher position; the one who accepted bribes and was dishonest was given the lower job of a porter; but the one who worked according to the wishes of his benefactor, with the attitude of wanting nothing for himself, ended up inheriting everything. This is our position too. What we experience are the fruits of our actions.

Only two things happen in life: we perform actions, and we enjoy their fruits. Positive actions bring good fruits, and negative actions bring bad fruits. An action isn't just what we do with our hands and feet. Thoughts are also actions. Speaking badly of others is a negative action and the result is misery.

But when we suffer we shouldn't grieve, thinking that we are sinners. Realizing that we are now experiencing the fruits of our past negative actions and that we shouldn't repeat them, we have to make the decision to fill the remaining moments of our life with positive actions. Don't condemn yourself as a sinner, a good for nothing, and so on. Leave everything to the Divine Will and live a life filled with compassion and service. This is the easiest way to attain peace in life.

My children, you must know that nothing happens according to our will. If we put out ten eggs to hatch, we won't see all of them hatching the way they are supposed to. Such things never happen. If our will prevailed, all ten eggs would hatch properly. We need to develop an attitude that leaves everything to God's will, the attitude of surrender. This should be our goal in life. Some ask, "Didn't your Krishna tell us to work without pay?" Not at all. What the Lord said was that the results of our actions may not be what we expect, so we will be disappointed if we set our hearts on the fruits of our actions. He didn't say we should work for no pay. He asked us to develop the attitude of surrender so that we will receive the right remuneration.

It is said that life is full of happiness and sorrow. Life is like the pendulum of a clock. The pendulum swings towards happiness but doesn't remain there; it oscillates back to sorrow. Spirituality harmonizes the two. Those who know how to swim can enjoy the waves of the ocean, while those who can't swim will collapse among the waves. If we know the principles of spirituality, we can maintain a smile through all circumstances in life, and we will surely reach the goal. Krishna counseled us on how we can reach the goal without collapsing along the way.

Marital love

Many different types of people come to see Amma, with different kinds of problems. Countless family problems arise out of really trivial matters. With a little patience, most of the problems could be solved. A troubled couple once came to Amma. The wife occasionally lost her mental balance slightly, and afterwards she didn't remember what she had said. This happened when she was under stress. But she really loved her husband. Knowing this, Amma said to the husband, "Son, you just have to be a little careful, that's all. When your wife says those things, you need to understand it is because of her illness, and you should forgive her. Slowly, she will get well." But the husband wouldn't accept that. He said, "Why should I yield to her? Isn't she my wife?" That was his attitude. And so, what happened? The family discord grew

Amma singing bhajans during her birthday celebration

worse and the wife's illness grew worse. Members of her family took her away, and the husband's life was shattered. He began to drink, and drank away all of his wealth. Life became a hell for him. If he had been more understanding towards his wife's illness and had been loving and patient towards her, none of this would have happened. So, my children, you should try to understand each situation as you go through life.

When Amma travels abroad, the people there sometimes ask, "Aren't women treated like slaves in India?" Amma tells them, "Not at all. In India, the relationship between husband and wife is grounded in love." It is said that a wife should have three qualities or aspects: that of a mother, a friend, and a wife. All three should be present. It is wrong to say that a wife should only have a particular quality. A woman shouldn't be like a tree grown in a flowerpot [her husband], because the tree in such a pot cannot grow sky high. Such a tree is weakened as its roots are trimmed away again and again. No bird can nest on its branches; no fruits can grow on it. A tree that is grown that way has no strength. But transplant it in the earth and you will see how it grows! You will see the fruition of its full potential.

Similarly, it is wrong to say that Woman is weak. She is strong! We just have to allow that strength to develop, allow that strength to discover itself instead of pruning its roots and confining it in a pot. A woman who develops to her fullest potential is like a huge, shade-giving tree that protects the family, society, and the country.

The husband and wife should become one. This is the attitude we should cultivate. Life is for sharing, not for possessing. This reminds Amma of a story. There was a man who was addicted to horse racing. He lost all his money on the horses and his business failed. He came home and said to his wife, "My business is ruined. What should we do now?"

She said, "From now on, avoid going to the races. We can manage to live on what we have."

"Okay, but then you have to give up buying expensive clothes," said the husband.

"All right," said the wife. "Also, we can no longer afford to employ a chauffeur, but you know how to drive."

"That's true," the husband agreed. "I will drive the car instead. Also, we can't afford the cook. I will assist you in the kitchen when you need help."

The wife happily agreed. They shared their lives in this way. They cut down on unnecessary expenses and made up for the loss they had suffered. This is the sort of life we need to build for ourselves.

Become one heart – become one. Life isn't meant for separating from one another, accusing each other, and saying, "Who are you to tell me what to do?"

Love is the wealth of India. Love is the very foundation of life. Ninety percent of the physical and mental problems we face stem from the pains and sorrows of the past. Each of us goes through life with many unhealed wounds. Medical science hasn't found a medicine that can cure those wounds. But there is a single cure for them all: that we open our hearts to each other.

Share your thoughts and feelings. Make an effort to recognize and fulfill each other's needs. My dear children, when mutual love and respect develop, your problems will recede. Love is the very ground of life. The cause of all our problems today is that we consciously or unconsciously ignore this. If the body needs food in order to grow, love is what the soul needs. Love supplies the baby with a strength and vitality that even breast milk cannot give.

So, my children, love one another and become one. This is Amma's wish. This is the ideal that Amma's children should foster.

Independence Day vow

Recently, India celebrated the fiftieth anniversary of its independence. Amma was abroad at that time. As we boarded each plane, going from city to city, those flying with Amma read the newspapers and sadly told her, "Amma, see what they've written about India! They say there's no progress at all, that there's starvation and pollution everywhere. They blow the problems out of proportion."

After three days in one place we would travel on to the next city. And in the newspapers on the planes everywhere, there was negative coverage about India, condemning the country. No one wrote anything positive. Finally, when we arrived in Europe, one paper had written, "You cannot say there is no progress in India. If we compare today with the day they gained independence, some progress has been made." After so many days we could finally read at least that.

So what is to be done as we celebrate the fiftieth anniversary of India's independence? Those of you who smoke should make a vow to give it up. Those who drink should make a decision to stop drinking. If you then unite and pool the money you previously spent on unnecessary things, we can replace the flimsy huts in the villages with real houses. We can provide destitute children with an education. There are so many children who have been forced to give up their schooling because they can't afford it. And Amma's teenage children can, for example, clean the gutters in the villages, and help free the atmosphere in and around the villages from pollution. If each of us tries in this way, our Bharat[30] will become a land of prosperity. We can turn this earth into a heaven. If the wealthy people in this country wish to save others, they can easily do so. But we hardly see anyone making an effort to do this. So, you should take the lead, my children!

---

[30] The traditional name of India.

As Amma has said before, be ready to act without having any expectations about the result. This doesn't mean that we have to renounce everything. Eat, talk, and sleep according to your needs; it is selfish to do these things in excess. It is said that people smoke and drink to experience happiness. But real happiness lies within and is not to be found in any external objects. Once we understand this, our addiction to such things will drop away. Then we can set aside that money to help the poor instead. We will then become eligible to receive God's grace and compassion.[31] Our lives will then be beneficial to others. My children, at least from now on, don't create the opportunity for people in other countries to accuse us in their papers! Make this vow today!

Amma has no interest in these birthday celebrations. Understand the purpose of your birth, my children! This is what is needed. If someone is genuinely willing to find out, it will give Amma far greater joy than any birthday celebration.

There are many who have come to Amma and have made the resolve to live a life of renunciation. Many stopped drinking or have given up their overly luxurious ways of life. As a result, we have had the good fortune to perform a great deal of service. If all of you, Amma's children, think in the same way, we can turn this earth itself into heaven. May you be blessed with the mental strength to do this.

---

[31] Editor's note: Amma says that God's grace is constantly pouring towards each of us, but that the grace can only be received if our hearts are open enough to receive it. To 'become eligible' in this context is the same as having an open heart.

Seeing all living beings as one's own Self

Amma's birthday message 1998

Salutations to all of you, who are verily the embodiments of love and the Supreme Self!

My children, let us begin by chanting the mantra *Lokah samastah sukhino bhavantu* together.

Many people are dying, not only in India but also in other parts of the world, because of floods, storms, landslides, and so on. Thousands of people experience terrible suffering because of wars between countries and within society. We haven't been able to find freedom from such miseries. Because of those circumstances, Amma doesn't like the idea of a celebration. However, Amma sees this celebration as an opportunity for all of us to come together and pray. Group prayer is highly valuable. With group prayer we can definitely bring about some changes to the miserable conditions of today. So, all of you, close your eyes, and with the prayer that all living beings everywhere be granted peace and happiness, repeat the mantra, *Om lokah samastah sukhino bhavantu.*

Sharing in life

This mantra was given to us by the *Rishis*, our ancestors. The mantra is chanted not only for our own benefit or for the benefit of our families. The meaning of the prayer is: "O Supreme Being, may all beings in all the worlds experience peace and happiness!" But, my children, we should ask ourselves if we have the broad-mindedness to be able to say this prayer.

Amma remembers a story. A man's wife died. He called a priest to conduct a prayer for the peace of his wife's soul. During the ceremony, the priest chanted the mantra, *Om lokah samastah sukhino bhavantu.* The husband didn't know the meaning of the mantra, so he asked the priest, "What is the meaning of the words that you just chanted?" The priest said, "It means, 'O Supreme Being, may all beings in all the worlds experience peace and happiness!'"

When he heard this, the husband said, "Didn't I ask you to come here to pray for my wife's soul? And, yet, the mantra you just chanted bears no hint of my wife's name or her soul!" The priest replied, "This is the prayer that my spiritual master taught me. In truth, it is when you pray for the whole world that your wife's soul experiences peace and upliftment. I don't know of any other way to pray."

The husband couldn't argue with this, but he said, "Can't you at least exclude my neighbors on the northern side of my property from the prayer? They have been very hostile towards us. You can pray for everyone except for them!"

My children, this is our attitude at present. But it is not an attitude that we should cultivate. No – this has to change. We have to change our whole outlook. These mantras are not to be uttered just by the tongue. They are principles to be practiced in our lives. Only then will that which our ancestors envisaged become real. Only then will our prayers bear fruit.

Meditation is good for worldly prosperity and for peace and liberation. Try to forget everything else as you meditate. Forget everything as you sit here and meditate for a little while. What do you gain if you think of family matters when you're sitting here? You will just waste your time. If you row a boat that remains tied to the river bank, you won't get to the other side.

Forget 'I' and 'mine' and surrender everything to God. God is everything. "Things don't go according to my own plans; isn't all this being done through Your will?" Recognize this and leave everything to God. Live in the present moment. We don't bring anything when we enter this world, nor do we take anything with us when we leave. We need to be aware of this and practice meditation. As soon you begin to repeat a mantra, you will get the benefit from it. It is like a fixed deposit in the bank. As soon as the deposit is made, your interest starts accruing. Don't think that meditation means only sitting with your eyes closed. A smiling face, a kind word, a compassionate glance, all this is part of meditation. Through meditation, our hearts should become compassionate. Only in such a heart can God shine! We should come to feel the suffering of others and share their suffering. This reminds Amma of a story.

A boy saw a sign in front of a store saying, "Puppies for sale!" He had a strong wish to buy a puppy, so he went into the shop. When he asked how much a puppy would cost, he was told between one hundred and two hundred dollars. "I don't have that much money, but can I at least see the puppies?" he asked. The shopkeeper couldn't refuse the boy. He blew a whistle and a litter of puppies and their mother came running in from the back of the store. The boy watched them with interest. When he saw the last puppy limping behind the others, he exclaimed, "Oh, look! What happened to that one?" The shopkeeper said, "That puppy was born with a lame leg. The vet said it won't heal." The boy watched with pity as the little puppy limped along, and asked, "Will you let me buy that one? I won't be able to pay you the full price now. I can pay part of it now, and the rest I'll pay in installments every month." The shopkeeper was surprised. "Why do you want that one, son? He won't be able to run around and play with you. Wouldn't you rather have one of the others?"

But the boy insisted on buying the lame puppy. "In that case, you don't have to pay anything for him," said the shopkeeper. "You can have him for free!"

"No, I want to buy him for the same price that you ask for the other puppies," said the boy firmly. When the shopkeeper asked why he was making such a fuss over a lame puppy, the boy lifted his leg up onto the table. Pulling up his trouser, he showed his artificial leg and said, "See this! I too am without a leg. So I'll share the heart of that puppy and he'll share mine! I'll understand his pain and he'll understand mine."

Even though Amma put it this way in the story, in order to understand the suffering of others it isn't necessary that we undergo the same suffering as they. We can feel the pain of others without going through what they are experiencing. So, try to think of the suffering of others as your own and the happiness of others as your own. This is the attitude we should have and cultivate. Amma knows it is hard. But try, my children!

There are a billion people in India. Only a quarter of them have adequate financial means. Half of the remaining people are small farmers and the rest are truly poor. There is really no reason for poverty to exist in this country. My children, the present situation can be changed if people like you were to make an effort to help. You know that we haven't asked anyone for help, nor have we collected any funds for the development of the ashram. The growth here has been due to your efforts, my children. Your hard work is the one thing that has paved the way for the service projects that we do. People like you and the residents of the ashram have worked for up to twenty-two hours a day. You have worked without any salary and without wishing for anything in return, reducing your requirements to just two pairs of clothes, and eating just two meals a day instead of three. You have dedicated all the money you have saved in this way to serving the world. The householder children are offering whatever services they can provide. Many women who used to buy ten saris a year are now buying only eight. People who used to drink and smoke have given up those habits. It is only because of people's selflessness that we are able to serve the poor and the suffering the way we do. If all of you were to put your minds to it in this way, we could definitely bring about at least a partial, if not a complete, change of the situation in this country. You may say, "But if you remove one drop of water from the ocean and pour it on land, surely that won't make a difference." But it will, because, after all there is now one drop less in the ocean! Likewise, if each one of us tries to do something good, we will certainly be able to see the difference in society. This is the attitude you should cultivate, my children!

Give up selfishness

It is because each of Amma's children is willing to live in accordance with the meaning of the mantra we are chanting, that we are able to selflessly do so many things that benefit society. But, today, selfishness rules the world. Selfishness is what lies behind the love that we see in the world. In a certain family the two sons got together and said to their father, "Dad, we children will look after you. Why don't you transfer the ownership of your house and all your property to us?" Trusting the sweet words of his children, the old man executed a deed transferring everything to them. He thought he'd let his sons take turns, and he'd live with each of them for two months at a time. When his property had been divided between his sons, he went and stayed with one of them. After only two weeks, his son and daughter-in-law's attitude towards him began to change. So, he moved out and went to stay with his other son. After just five days, he couldn't continue living there either because he couldn't bear the cutting remarks he received from his daughter-in-law. He was crying all the time. Finally, he took refuge at an ashram. Hearing the man's story, the spiritual master at the ashram offered him some advice. A month later, the father returned to his sons carrying a box. The sons eagerly wanted to know what the box contained. When they pressed the old man, he said, "I have converted a part of my wealth into gold, and I keep it in this box. But I won't give this box to anyone until I die. When I am dead, any of you can have it." His sons' attitude towards him changed the moment they heard this. They had no words with which to express the love they suddenly felt for their father. They and their wives pleaded with him, "Come and stay with us, Dad! Please come to our house!" They offered him greater and greater hospitality. Finally, the day came when the old man died. After the funeral, the sons hastened to open the box which they had been eyeing all along. With great excitement, they removed the lid. The box was full of ordinary stones!

My children, this is the kind of love we get from the world. If we expect something from the world, we will have occasion for nothing but tears.

My children, the effort made by all of you is the source of all the success we have made here. You are my children! You are Amma's only wealth. Amma has nothing of her own. All that we see today comes from your selflessness. So, remember one thing in particular, my dear children. If even just a speck of selfishness manages to enter your minds, you should get rid of it somehow. A single spark is enough to start a wildfire that reduces a whole forest to ashes – and that is what selfishness is like. Just a little of it is enough to completely rob us of our peace.

Now and then women come here weeping, with two or three infants on their hips. When Amma asks them what the trouble is, they say, "Amma, I set out with my children to commit suicide. Then I heard about Amma, so we came here." When Amma wants to know more, the woman says, "My husband drinks. He's addicted to drugs. Because of the drinking, he never went to work on time, so he lost his job. Still he didn't stop drinking. In the end, he sold the house, our property, my jewelry, everything. We couldn't afford even a single meal. I never saw a smiling face anywhere. Everyone hated us. Everywhere I saw only disdainful glances. In the end, all I could see clearly ahead was the path to death. So I set out towards that path with my babies. But instead we ended up here with you, Amma!"

Amma will tell you something; those men are consuming the tears and the blood of their loved ones, not alcohol or drugs.

The angler throws the fishing line in the water and waits. The fish takes the bait and thinks, "Great! I have found enough food for today!" It doesn't realize it is in the jaws of death.

The dog takes a bone in its mouth, chews on it eagerly and savors the blood that comes out. Only later does it realize that the blood it tasted came from its own lacerated gums. Happiness is not to be found in objects. Happiness exists within us. My children, you need to understand this. Those of you who strive only for your own happiness should think of your families, at least for a moment! Those of you who smoke five cigarettes a day, try to cut it down and smoke two less! By reducing it little by little, you can eliminate the habit completely. Likewise, those who drink should try to stay away from that atmosphere. Regain your strength with the knowledge that happiness doesn't really exist in the drinking. A courageous person is he or she who looks for joy within. My children, don't be slaves to cigarettes or alcohol. Those who become slaves to such things have no courage. They are cowards. The really courageous people are those who have gained control over their minds. We don't need to lean on anything. We should be able to stand on our own. We should make our every breath beneficial to others. You should make this inner resolution. This is all that Amma desires.

The way to face experiences

We confront the experiences of life in three different ways:

1. We try to run away from the situations.

2. We try to change the circumstances, believing that such a change will solve all our problems.

3. We curse our circumstances and proceed somehow.

We cannot avoid problems by running away from them; in fact, the problems may double. A story comes to mind. There was a man who heard that his uncle was about to visit him. He decided to leave the house because his uncle, who was a soldier, was in the habit of telling war stories for hours at a stretch. Not wanting to waste all that time, the nephew made his escape along a path behind the house. But as he walked along the path, he suddenly saw his uncle on that same path from the opposite direction! As soon as his eyes fell on his nephew, the uncle stopped and started talking. The conversation went on and on, right there on the path. After a while the nephew felt very hot and thirsty, and his feet were hurting. But there was no water available, no shady tree in sight, and no bench to sit on. It occurred to him that if he had stayed at home he would now be sitting comfortably in the cool shade with his uncle, and he would have access to plenty of water. From this story we can see that if we try to run away from situations, it could cause twice as many problems.

The second approach is to change the environment. In a certain home there is no peace at all. The family members think there's something wrong with the house. "Perhaps we should pull the house down and rebuild it. Or should we buy another house? Or perhaps we need to get a new TV and a few more things and decorate the house. We could install an air-conditioner." But none of this will solve the problems. There are people who cannot sleep even in the luxury of an air-conditioned room. They have to take sleeping pills. The reason is that their problems are in their minds. Spirituality is the art of 'air-conditioning' the mind. The problems of life do not disappear if we just make some changes in our surroundings. It's not that we shouldn't change the outer environment. Amma is saying that we need to change our mental makeup as well. This is what spirituality teaches us.

Changing the environment doesn't put an end to the problems. A couple used to fight with each other constantly. Finally, they couldn't live together any longer, and they divorced. After some time they both remarried. But each of them soon discovered that they had simply married their former spouse in a different form! The individuals were new, but their own minds hadn't changed at all. As long as our minds haven't changed, we won't free ourselves from our problems by changing the external conditions.

The third way we deal with difficult situations in our lives is to complain about the situations and go on. Someone with a stomach ache keeps complaining to everyone in the house, "Mom! Dad! I have a pain in my stomach! Brother, sister, I can't bear this pain!" Finally, everyone who goes near that person also gets a stomach ache. By endlessly complaining about our problems, we end up destroying the peace of others as well.

But there is a fourth way. There is way to overcome difficult situations, and that is to change our state of mind. This is the only way to truly find joy. It is impossible to change the external environment completely to suit our needs. So we need to change our state of mind to suit the environment. This is possible only through spirituality.

This is where spiritual texts become relevant. What did Lord Krishna show Arjuna?[32] Krishna didn't change the state of the external world; he transformed the state of Arjuna's mind. Had he wanted to, he could have created a tornado or a deluge and destroyed the unrighteous Duryodhana and his followers. He

---

[32] Arjuna was one of the five Pandava brothers. Lord Krishna's advice to Arjuna at the start of the Mahabharata war is known as the Bhagavad Gita, and contains the essence of spiritual wisdom for our day-to-day life.

could have used any method to destroy them. He could have secured everything for the Pandavas. Krishna had the power to do this. But he didn't alter the outer circumstances at all; instead, he changed Arjuna's attitude towards the world. He taught him to understand the nature of life and how to face everything in life. We need to develop our minds in such a way that we can pray for the peace and harmony of the whole world.

Remember the scene from the Ramayana: Lord Rama entered the hall where Sita was about to choose a husband.[33] As soon as the people of Mithila saw Rama, they began to pray, "How handsome and strong he is, and he is blessed with all good qualities! God, please give him the strength to string that bow!" As Rama entered the hall, all the kings who had assembled there hoping to win Sita's hand began to curse Rama in their minds. "Why did he have to come here now? Will I miss my chance because of him? It seems doubtful that I will get to marry Sita. If only he would go away!" And when Sita saw Rama, she began to pray: "O God, why did you make such a heavy bow? Can't you decrease its weight a little?" Hers was a prayer to change the circumstances.

But the prayer of the people of Mithila was the proper one. They had the right attitude. They didn't pray for the circumstances to change. They prayed, "Give Rama the strength to string that bow!" Similarly, whatever the situation, we should pray only for the courage to confront it. But our prayer shouldn't be a childish one.

A boy went to a temple and prayed, "God, please make China the capital of America!" A person nearby overheard this and asked, "Why are you praying like that, child?" The boy said, "I wrote in

---

[33] Sita's father, King Janaka of Mithila, declared that he would give his daughter in marriage only to the king or prince who was able to string the great bow that originally belonged to Lord Shiva. Many royal suitors had assembled hoping to try to accomplish the feat and win Sita's hand.

the exam that the capital of America is China! But I was wrong. So I'm praying to God to make my answer right!"

This is childish. We shouldn't cultivate such childishness. But we should develop a childlike heart, childlike innocence. Childishness is lack of discrimination; it makes us immature. Suppose you take swimming lessons. If your swimming teacher always stays close to you, you won't learn how to swim by yourself. We ourselves need to find the strength to survive in whatever circumstances we find ourselves in life, and the only way to do this is to change our mental condition. Don't waste your life blaming the external conditions and feeling dejected at your inability to change them. There are those who travel in fancy cars, but if they have no peace of mind, what is the use of having a fancy car?

Changing the external conditions isn't enough. There are people who commit suicide in their air-conditioned rooms. On the other hand, if we transform our minds, we can face any situation with a smile. Instead of leaning on others for solace, we should develop faith in ourselves. Only then will we find comfort and satisfaction. So, changing our present mental attitude is the first step. This is what we should pray for.

Share the goodness

My children, we are not isolated islands. Each of us is a link in the chain of life. Our every action influences others whether we are aware of it or not; and we, in turn, are influenced by others. This is why it is said that we have to practice attentive awareness with every word and deed.

A man stepped onto a bus and was surprised to see that the conductor was so calm and cheerful. The conductor smiled at everyone, made sure the bus came to a halt at each stop, waited until everyone had boarded properly before ringing the bell signaling for the bus to go, and sold the tickets with great efficiency. The crowded bus and the behavior of the passengers didn't affect his mood at all. The passenger noticed this and asked the conductor, "How can you act so calmly and smile the way you do on such a crowded bus? I haven't come across this on any other bus. What's your secret?" The conductor smiled and said, "There's no big secret. This is simply the lesson life has taught me. I used to work in an office, and I had to travel to work by bus. The bus often stopped some distance away from the actual bus stop. I would run, and by the time I reached the bus, it had started again and I missed it. Or the conductor would ring the bell for the bus to start just as I touched the bus, and it would be difficult for me to climb on without falling. The conductor usually didn't bother to return my change, and if I asked for it, he'd give it resentfully; or if I didn't have the exact change he'd be angry. When these things happened, I almost lost control over my mind. But I reminded myself that I'd have to catch the same bus the next day, and I somehow managed to control myself. So, I'd arrive at the office suppressing all this anger.

I wasn't friendly at all, nor did I smile at anyone. So everyone started being unfriendly towards me. Because of this, I couldn't pay the proper attention to my work. I felt so tense that I made a lot of mistakes, and I was scolded by the manager. All this would remain within me when I came home in the evenings, and I would take it out on my family. I'd get angry at the children and quarrel with my wife. There was no peace in the atmosphere. I no longer showed my children any affection, nor did I open my heart to my wife. I became a loner both at home and in society.

"Then one day when I reached the bus stop, the bus pulled out and was leaving. When the conductor saw me, he rang the bell and stopped the bus. He waited until I had boarded completely before signaling for the bus to start again. There were no empty seats in the bus, but that conductor gave me his own seat. I felt an inexpressible joy. I was very tired and fell asleep on the way.

Just before we arrived at my stop, the conductor woke me up so that I could get off. I had never met that conductor before. I can't describe the solace that his kindness gave me. Imagine the relief you feel when you are tormented by thirst and someone offers you a glass of cool water. The relief I felt was even greater than that. It was with unprecedented joy that I left the bus and walked to the office. And there, everyone smiled at me, which was unusual. I was able to do my work with great care that day, and the manager praised me. That day, I was very friendly towards those working under me. This made them happy and they opened up to me. And they became very friendly towards those who visited the office that day. At home, I was able to be loving and open with my wife and children. There was a festive air in the house. I enjoyed it so much I forgot everything else. I became aware of the changes that had taken place in everyone around me because of the transformation in me – the transformation of one person.

"From then on, I began paying special attention to my own behavior. I became convinced that we are given back exactly what we give. I cannot insist that others become good before I myself become good. I learned that I could better myself even if the others didn't do so; that if I, myself, became good, others would also begin to change. Later, when I took this job on the bus, I remembered the conductor who taught me this great lesson. I made a vow to show people respect when I interacted with them. I made a firm resolve to play my part in nurturing love and a sense of kinship in the world. The experience I had that day when everything changed remains a great lesson for me." And that is the story the conductor told.

My children, society is made up of individuals. The thoughts and actions of each individual shape the culture of the people. Instead of thinking, "I'll become good when the others change," we should first attempt to transform ourselves. If our own mental outlook truly changes, we'll be able to see goodness everywhere in the world. When a change takes place in us, it is reflected in others as well. My children, always remember that we receive only what we give.

The heart pumps blood into all the cells of the body. The cells get nutrition in this way. The blood then flows back into the heart. If there is any obstacle to this, life itself becomes threatened. Like the heart, we need to learn not only to receive but also to give back. Only when we give, do we receive in return. In the chain of life, a deficiency in one link will affect the others. We need to understand that our every smile, word, and deed has the power to spread sunshine to the lives of many others. So, we need to make sure that our actions create joy and contentment not only for us but also for others. We shouldn't withdraw in disappointment when we see evil in the world, nor should the wrongs of others influence us to do wrong.

My children, instead of blaming the darkness, make an effort to light at least one little lamp. If that isn't possible, try not to create any suffering or difficulties for others. You may wonder how this can be done. The easy way is to make every action an offering to the Supreme Being. Think of every action as a form of worship. Then, our actions will make both us and others happy, and will benefit us and others as well.

Amma remembers what one son told her several years ago. He wanted to study medicine, but he didn't get admitted to medical school because his grades were lower than required by just one point. He didn't do anything for a while after that. Then, on the insistence of his family, he applied for a job in a bank and was accepted. He became a bank clerk. He came to Amma after that and said, "Amma, I am always very angry. I cannot smile or show any love towards the customers, no matter who they are. So I don't think I'll be able to continue with this job." He said this with a lot of anguish.

Amma asked him, "Son, if your dearest friend were to send someone to you, how would you behave towards that person?"

"I would smile and be affectionate."

"So then you would behave nicely. And what if Amma herself were to send someone to see you at the bank, how would you act?"

"Because Amma had sent that person, I would be very loving!"

Then Amma said to him, "From now on, try to imagine that everyone who comes to you has been sent to you by God. If you can do this, then, surely, you will change!"

After that a change did indeed take place in that son. He began to see his job as a way of serving God. He was happy and shared his contentment with those who came to him. By performing our actions as worship of God, not only we, but society as a whole, will benefit. This is the attitude we should nurture.

Effort combined with grace

My children, two things happen in life: we perform actions and we experience their fruits. Our lives will become relatively peaceful and harmonious if we know what our attitude should be when we perform our actions and enjoy their fruits.

We often find that what we really expect doesn't happen, and that what we don't expect comes true. The fruit of an action depends not only on the action itself, but also on many other factors. Only if all of those factors come together do we get the result that we expect. Only the performance of the action is under our control. We should perform the action to the best of our ability, without worrying about the result. This is what Lord Krishna advises in the Bhagavad Gita. This doesn't mean we should work for no pay. It means that if we act without expecting the result, we will be able do the action well. Then the fruits of our actions will come naturally to us.

Even if we do very well on an exam, we may not get the expected result if the professor grading the test, or the clerk copying the grades, doesn't pay proper attention to their work. A boy studied hard and did well in the exam. He expected to get a top rank. But when the results were announced, he had just barely passed. However, he didn't allow himself to be dejected by this. He took certain steps to get his answers graded again. When the paper was graded a second time, he got a much higher rank. When an investigation was made as to why this had happened, it was revealed that the professor who graded the exam the first time had been deeply disturbed at the time. His wife had run away with another man, and because he was so upset about this, he wasn't able to evaluate the examination papers properly. This is why Amma says that success in our exams is not decided by our effort alone, no matter how much we study and how well we answer the questions.

No matter how watchful we are while crossing a road, we could still be injured if a driver happens to be careless. This is why it is said that for all the factors that control the result of an action to be in our favor, we need God's grace. The easiest way to achieve this is to perform every action as worship of God.

When we perform a *puja*, we naturally try to ensure that all the articles we use for the *puja* be of the highest quality. We never use rotten fruit, withered flowers, or dirty utensils. When we do everything with this attitude, in due course we will only be capable of performing positive actions. Negative actions will cease, because how can you perform a negative action if you are dedicating it to God?

The most important attitude of a person who performs a *puja* is humility. So, when we perform every action as a *puja*, with the right attitude, we won't be able to exhibit any arrogance or pride.

118

If we succeed in a certain action, we will see it as God's grace; we won't boast that the success is due to our own ability.

At the end of the *puja* we receive *prasad*.[34] So, with the attitude that our actions are a form of worship, we accept the fruits of our actions as *prasad*. The humility we have while performing the action must remain with us while we experience the fruit of the action as well. We don't look for defects or deficiencies in the *prasad*.

This doesn't mean that if we fail we should just sit around lazily and accept our failure as God's *prasad*. If there is a possibility of success, we should try again; and if we fail again, we can accept that as Divine Will. When we think of our success as divine grace we won't be boastful; we won't revel in our success and get overly excited to the exclusion of everything else. And if we happen to fail, we don't feel shattered and sink to the ground. In those who perceive their failures as God's will, the feeling of being good for nothing does not arise. When we fail we should think that it is simply what we deserve at this particular point in time. We should think that another *prarabdha* (a fruit of some past action) has been avoided in this way. We need to treat the experience as a lesson in life and accept that there is something to be learned from it.

By using our power of discrimination, we can turn any action in our favor. And when we approach our actions with the right attitude, we can also avoid getting bored. When our enthusiastic effort is combined with divine grace, victory will certainly be on our side. Whatever happens, we should never give up hope. God is always with those who strive. Victory is with them as well.

---

[34] Any blessed items, for example, food or flowers.

Amma praying during her birthday celebration

Spirituality in practical life

Amma's birthday message 1999

Salutations to all of Amma's children, who are verily the embodiments of love and the Supreme Self!

In this age, speeches and discourses are being held throughout the country. Spiritual discourses, cultural discourses, political speeches, religious talks, talks against religion – everyone has some subject or the other to speak about. Everyone has the authority to make speeches on every subject under the sun. This seems to be the general attitude.

A story comes to mind about the student who says to his friends, "We have a fantastic professor. You give him any subject, and he'll speak on it for hours. Even if you give him a topic on something insignificant, he'll talk for more than five hours." Hearing this, one of his friends replies, "You are saying that your professor speaks for more than five hours if given a subject to speak on. But our neighbor, you don't have to give him a subject, and yet he'll keep talking for days on end!"

This is what many speeches are like today. Speeches are not what we need; we need actions! It is with our own lives that we should demonstrate what we have to say. Good words and deeds are certainly beneficial; they can never be meaningless. An incident from the Mahabharata comes to mind.

It was the time when the Pandavas and Kauravas were young and were being taught by their great teacher, Dronacharya. The first lesson was about forbearance. One day the teacher called all the disciples and asked them to recite what they had learned so far. Each of them recited the lessons from memory. Finally, it was Yudhisthira's turn. He repeated just one line. When the teacher asked, "Is that all you have learned?" Yudhisthira reluctantly replied, "Forgive me, Sir. I have more or less learned the first lesson, but the second one I haven't learned at all." When he heard this, Drona couldn't control his anger. He had expected Yudhisthira to do better than the others – and, yet, while the others were reciting entire lessons, Yudhisthira was saying he could barely remember two lines. In his anger, Drona grabbed a stick and beat Yudhisthira with it until the stick broke into small pieces. But even after receiving those blows, Yudhisthira remained cheerful and the smile on his face didn't fade. Drona's anger cooled when he saw this, and he regretted what he had done. He said affectionately, "My child, you are a prince! If you had wanted to, you could have punished me by having me thrown into prison. But you didn't do that. You were not angry at all! Is there anyone in this world who has your patience? There is such greatness in you!" When he turned around, Drona saw the palm leaf on which Yudhisthira's lessons were written. The first line read, 'Never lose your patience,' while the second line read, 'Always tell only the truth!'

When Drona's glance fell on Yudhisthira's face again, he thought those lines on the palm leaf were shining through the young prince's eyes. He grabbed hold of Yudhisthira's hands and, with his eyes brimming with tears, he said, "Yudhisthira! When I was teaching you, I merely mouthed some words. And the other boys repeated those words like parrots. You were the only one who really learned the lessons. How great you are, my son! Despite having taught this for so long, I wasn't able to learn even a single line. I couldn't control my anger, nor was I patient!" Yudhisthira responded, "Forgive me, Master, but I *did* feel a little angry towards you." Drona now realized that his disciple had learned the second lesson as well.

Those who don't succumb when they hear a little praise are very rare. Even if they have a little anger in them, they won't want to show it. But look at Yudhisthira. He didn't show any reluctance in admitting that he had been slightly angry. This means that he had also learned the second lesson. A lesson is complete only when it is practiced in life. The true disciple is he or she who really tries to do this.

We also need patience in life because patience is the very foundation of life. If we force open a bud, we will never know the beauty or fragrance of the flower. Only if it opens naturally will we experience this. Similarly, if we wish to enjoy the beauty of life, we cannot do without patience. For those who want their lives to be filled with happiness, patience is the most important quality they need.

It is sometimes said that fire is the deity of speech. The nature of fire is heat, light, and smoke. Just as fire gives heat and light, each word of ours should give energy and knowledge to others. But it shouldn't taint their minds the way smoke blackens a room. Today, if we listen to our words, we can tell that fire is indeed the deity behind speech, because what our words emit is heat and smoke. Wisdom and light are totally absent. Each word of ours should create a transformation in the listeners. It should bring bliss to others. We should be role models for others. Each word we utter should have that power. Simplicity and humility should shine forth in our words. But, today, if we sift through our words, we won't find a trace of humility.

Our words are pervaded with the attitude that we want to be better than others. Even the lowliest person tries to pose as great in front of others. We don't pay attention to the fact that a person's greatness actually lies in his or her humility. We don't realize that if we act like that, we become fools in the eyes of others.

An army major was promoted to the rank of colonel. On the day he assumed charge of the new post, a man came to visit him. As soon as the man entered the office, the colonel picked up the phone with an air of importance and started talking. "Hello, is that President Clinton? How are you? I took charge just today. There are so many files to go through. OK, I'll call later. Please give my regards to Hillary." After talking like this for a while, he put the phone down. The visitor just stood there and waited very courteously. With an air of arrogance the colonel said to him, "Yes, what do you want?"

The man said politely, "Excuse me, Sir. I'm here to connect the phone. This is a new phone that was put in yesterday and the line hasn't been connected."

Who was the fool here? We don't see that we become fools like this several times a day. That's all there is to it. Those who try to display their own importance actually become fools in the eyes of others.

Controlling anger

Another thing we should pay special attention to in life is controlling our anger. Anger is like a knife that is sharp at both ends. It cuts the one it is aimed at as well as the one who is holding it. How turbulent our minds become when we are angry with someone! The mind becomes so disturbed that we cannot sit, stand, or lie down in peace. Our blood heats up. This paves the way for all the diseases we didn't have until now. In the heat of our anger, we don't recognize the changes that take place within us.

Many people smile at someone only after first calculating, "If I smile, will it turn that person into an acquaintance? Will he or she ask me for money? Does that person need money right now?" They'll smile only after considering such things carefully. But this is not the case with anger. In an instant, we get totally carried away by anger. However, we do try to control ourselves in certain situations. Normally, people don't flare up at a superior, because they know they'll end up paying for it. Our superior may be talking about transferring us to another location, or not granting us the promotion we were meant to get, or even terminating our job. Under such circumstances, most people exercise the utmost self-control. Those who cannot do so land in trouble, and others see this as a lesson for themselves. But few people exercise any control when they get angry at their subordinates. This is where self-control is truly needed, because our subordinates cannot talk back. They are dependent on us. They may not show any reaction outwardly, but they'll feel hurt, and they will think, "O God, I'm forced to hear all this abuse for mistakes I haven't committed! Don't You see the truth, God?" Those waves of sorrow emanating from their hearts will become a curse to us, and it won't be easy to escape from it.

Some people don't pass their exams even though they have studied very hard. And there are those who attend several job interviews but cannot get employment. The reason could be that they have hurt someone's feelings very badly. The heartfelt prayer of that individual has turned into an obstacle, like a curse, and this blocks the divine grace that should be flowing to the person.

This doesn't mean that we shouldn't reprimand someone when it is needed. It is important to correct mistakes when we see them; being outwardly loving and gentle may not work with everyone, in which case we need to act in a serious way. But this shouldn't be directed at the individual as such, only at the wrong action. We shouldn't needlessly be stern with anyone. We need to be careful so that our words and deeds do not wound anyone.

In some families, we see deaths taking place in successive years. In other families, a series of accidents take place. For some young women, no matter how many marriage proposals they receive, none of them are suitable. In some families, no children are born, while in other families people die at a young age. There are families in which all the women become widows in their thirties or forties. The only reason that can be given for this is that these circumstances are the fruits of previous *karma*.

This is why Amma says, again and again, that with every deed, word, and glance of ours, and even with every thought, we have to be very careful. Every one of our thoughts, words, and deeds has its own consequences. Every good or bad action of ours affects many others. Amma remembers a story in this context.

The court jester was telling the king a story, and as he proceeded with the tale, he cracked several jokes. But the king didn't understand the jokes. He thought the jester was probably making fun of him. The king got angry and hit the jester hard. The poor jester was in terrible pain. He gnashed his teeth in anger, but as it was the king who had hit him, he didn't dare to utter a word in his own defense. However, try as he might, he couldn't control his anger, because he had been hit for no real reason. So he turned around and slapped the man standing next to him. The man asked the court jester, "What did you do that for? I haven't done anything to you, so why did you slap me?"

"So what!" said the jester. "Just pass it on to the person next to you! Life is like a big wheel," he said. "As it turns, we can see each of us getting what we deserve. So don't hesitate to pass it along!"

Love – the fragrance of life

This is what we see around us even today. We take out our anger and vengeance on those who happen to be standing nearby, even though they may not know anything at all about the situation. There is no doubt that what we give will come back to us, either today or tomorrow. In the West, if a husband beats his wife, he is often beaten right back. But that is not the case in India. Our ancestors have taught us that the husband is a visible form of God. But what is the wife to the husband? Many husbands now see their wives as dumping grounds for their anger. The wife bears the beating and the verbal abuse, and suppresses her own anger. At that moment her son comes home from school. He runs into the house and jumps up and down with excitement about his plans to play with his friends that evening. But as soon as she sees him, the mother's anger doubles. She catches hold of him and says, "Can't you walk, instead of run? Stop jumping like that! Why did you get your clothes so dirty?"

And she beats him till her anger abates. That poor child! What wrong did he do? There was only joy and laughter in his world. But did his mother understand this? In a society that is full of selfishness and ego, the small world of the children – a world filled with play and laughter – gets crushed.

Life should blossom into total laughter. This is religion. This is spirituality. This is real prayer. God is the innocent, spontaneous smile that blossoms from within. This is the greatest prize we can give the world. But in today's world this laughter has become foreign to people. The world today knows only the smile filled with selfishness, spite, and artificiality. That is not a smile; it is just the stretching of the lips, because there is no heart present. This is a sin, a form of violence, a betrayal of the Self. We need to recover the child's world, a world that is filled with laughter and playfulness. There is a child slumbering within each of us. Without awakening this child, we cannot evolve.

Today, our bodies have grown upwards and outwards, but our minds haven't grown. We have to become like children in order for our minds to grow and become as expansive as the universe – for only a child can grow. We need to have the purity and humility of a child. Humility is the quality that makes us grow as expansive as the universe. This is why it is said that you can become a hero only if you first become a 'zero.'

Many people complain that it isn't possible to evolve by trying to do good in today's world. But each moment of life is an opportunity to do good. For those who wish to do good, each moment can be useful, and those who postpone it are deceiving themselves.

What husband would say to his wife, "I will love you at ten o'clock tomorrow morning or at five in the afternoon."?

If someone were to say that, those words would make it clear that there's no love there at all. Love isn't something that appears or is added later. Love is here *now*. Love and faith are the beauty of life. But it is people's nature to throw stones at love and faith wherever those qualities are found. This has to change. Love is the rose that lends a pure fragrance to life. No one should throw stones at it.

Modern people focus on reason and intellect, and often hold the view that love and faith are blind concepts. But Amma says that reason is blind – because when there is nothing but logic and reason, life itself withers away. So, our focus should be on love, mutual trust, and faith. Imagine a society built on reason and intellect alone! In such a society there will be only machines that look good, move by themselves, and talk. This is why Amma says that love and faith are the foundation of life.

Manure and fertilizer should be placed at the roots of the rose bush. Don't heap them on top of the fragrant blossoms and ruin the sweet scent! Apply reason and intellect where they belong. Don't allow reason and intellect to ruin the love and faith that give beauty and fragrance to life!

The pilgrimage to Sabarimala[35] is an example of how countless people are uplifted by love and faith. For forty-one days, the pilgrims give up drinking and bad company, stop boastful talk, and live a celibate life with a sense of right and wrong, and they chant a single mantra, *Swamiye Sharanam* (The Lord is my only refuge!). At least during that time, the family and society experience freedom from the effects of alcohol and drugs. And, yet, people compete in aiming arrows of criticism even at this pilgrimage and its traditions. The argument is that the people

---

[35] A pilgrim center in Kerala with a famous Lord Ayyappan temple.

are merely being duped, their faith is being exploited, and so forth. But people don't see the practical side. We must carefully examine things and criticize only when it is appropriate. And the criticism shouldn't be blind; it shouldn't be such that it kills what is positive. Only through love and faith can we realize the principle of the Self.

Today, love is the subject of hundreds of movies, novels, and songs. It is the favorite subject of most writers, but love isn't born out of mere reading or writing. It is difficult to find true love in today's world. Even the relationship between husband and wife is becoming mechanical. Life itself has become boring.

Amma is reminded of a story. A husband and wife were sleeping on a cot in the courtyard in front of their house. Suddenly, a whirlwind came and lifted them up along with the cot, and carried them away. They were put down on a spot a hundred kilometers away. Luckily, they were not hurt. The wife began to sob. The husband asked, "Why are you weeping, dear? Look! We landed safely, didn't we? No harm has been done. We didn't even cut ourselves. So why are you weeping?"

The wife replied, "I'm not weeping out of sadness; I'm weeping because I'm so happy!"

"Why are you so happy?"

The wife answered, "Isn't this the first time we've traveled together since we got married? After all this time! I couldn't help weeping when I thought about it."

This is what family life is like nowadays!

Love is the union of hearts. Love is the act of hearts merging and becoming one. Love is the feeling, "I and my life belong to my beloved!" Love is total surrender. But total surrender and everlasting love cannot be felt towards objects that change. Only towards the unchanging Supreme Spirit is it possible to feel love and a sense of surrender.

True love is the emotion of the heart towards the Supreme Spirit, an irrepressible longing for God. Only through surrender to God can we experience this love, this selflessness and complete bliss. We need to dedicate our lives fully to God. This is complete surrender, and without it, true happiness isn't possible.

The circumstances are complex

The basis of success lies not in our actions, for it is only through divine grace that we succeed in anything. When we attempt to do something, many factors are involved in addition to the action we perform. Only when all the factors are favorable can we get the desired result. However careful we are when crossing the road, we know that if a driver is careless we could get run over. Suppose we are driving a car and we carefully observe all the traffic rules. Still, a drunken driver coming from the opposite direction may collide with us.

Many things are known today, but we still don't understand the true nature of the world. Only by understanding the real nature of the world will we experience peace of mind. We are surrounded by everything we need to increase our physical comforts, but no matter how much we change the material circumstances, basic changes aren't taking place within.

Amma remembers an incident. A gentleman from India was invited to visit America. All the arrangements were made for his visit. When he reached the house where he was going to stay, his host welcomed him. She asked, "What would you like to drink?" Her solicitous enquiry pleased him. He said, "Some tea would be fine." "What kind of tea would you like? Caffeinated or decaffeinated? Or would you prefer some lemon tea? Or perhaps some ginger tea would be better." She named many different kinds of tea the guest had never heard of. All he had tasted in life was ordinary black tea with the standard milk and sugar. He was very confused. "Why is she asking all this?" he thought.

"I'd like some ordinary tea," he said.

The lady went into the kitchen and came back again. "Excuse me, but would you like your tea with sugar, artificial sugar, or without sugar? There's even a completely natural sugar!"

At this stage, the visitor nearly lost his patience. "I just want tea."

She asked again, "Would like your tea with milk or without milk? And should it be whole milk, low-fat or fat-free milk?"

By now he was quite upset. "Oh God! Just a glass of water will do!"

The lady quickly asked, "Do you want filtered water or spring water? Or do you prefer sparkling water?" By this time, his patience was totally gone. He walked into the kitchen, poured himself a glass of water from the sink and drank it. That was all he needed. But how many questions were put to him!

Even if our need is small, there may be many ways to satisfy it. And today those ways are ever increasing. There are, for example, so many ways to reach a place; all types of vehicles are available. We can reach there at whatever speed we like. But, despite all of these conveniences, when there is some difficulty or suffering or sadness, none of those options can help us; we can only suffer. No other way appears before us. This is where spirituality becomes relevant. There is a way to gain freedom from suffering and sadness. Why did this suffering happen to us? What is the reason for our struggle? We should try to understand the real reason, because if we don't grasp it, the suffering will continue.

A young woman's boyfriend comes to her and says, "How beautiful you are! Being close to you makes me so happy. I can't even imagine life without you!" She feels overjoyed when she hears this. But not long thereafter he says, "Don't even come near me! I am allergic to you!" Hearing this she collapses with sorrow. She doesn't realize that this is the nature of the world, and so she suffers.

What is the nature of the world? Love is tied to an object. We love the cow for her milk. When she stops giving milk, she is sold to the butcher. This is what it will be like if we depend on the world. The world won't be with us in times of sorrow. When sorrow comes, ask the question, "Why did this happen to me?" If we can discover the answer to this question in every crisis, we will know how to proceed. The one who is trying to cross the river now will later be able to cross an entire ocean if that effort is constantly maintained. The problems that arise from time to time in life actually make us stronger. They are the situations that God brings about to increase our strength. If our foot is pricked by a small thorn, we will pay more attention when we walk, and that may save us from falling into a deep ditch. We should remember this and try to hold on to the Supreme Being.

You cannot become a weightlifting champion if you never lift anything but small weights. You have to put in the required effort to become a champion – twenty-five kilos at first, then thirty, forty, fifty and so on, slowly increasing the weights. Similarly, only those who persist in their efforts achieve victory in any area. If you practice only using light weights, you will slip and fall when trying to lift heavy weights. At present, we don't know how to stand on our own. If that which we are leaning on happens to shift a little, we are sure to fall. Spirituality gives us the practice to remain firmly rooted in ourselves.

Let the divine will prevail

My children, we often say, "It happened only because I thought about it, because of my will!" But is it really because of our will that anything happens?

"I'm coming out right now," someone calls from inside the house, and then that person takes just one step, has a heart attack, and collapses! If our will alone had any real power, wouldn't that person have been able to go outside the house as promised? We need to understand this and leave everything to the Divine Will.

There is a story about Radha and the *gopis* in this context.[36] When Lord Krishna left Vrindavan and went to Mathura, it made the *gopis* extremely sad to be separated from him. They sat on the banks of the Yamuna River, sharing their grief.

"Krishna didn't take us with him. If he comes back, we shouldn't let him go away again," said one of the *gopis*. "When the Lord comes back, I will ask for a boon," said another *gopi*.

"What will you to ask for?"

"That I shall be able to play with the Lord forever – that will be my request."

A third *gopi* said, "Can I ask for a boon, too?"

"What would that be?"

"That the Lord will eat butter out of my hands![37] That's the boon I'll ask for."

Another *gopi* said, "He should take me with him to Mathura, that's what I'll ask for."

"I want to be allowed to fan him always," said another.

The *gopis* noticed that Radha hadn't uttered a word, and one of them said, "Radha, why aren't you saying anything? What boon will you ask for? Tell us, Radha!"

They kept insisting until Radha finally said, "If I feel a desire for anything, I will offer that desire at the feet of my Lord. Whatever his will is, that is also my will. His happiness is my happiness."

So, leave everything to God's will. We cannot even be sure that we will be able to take our next breath; it is not under our

---

[36] The gopis were cowherd girls and milk maids who lived in Vrindavan. They were Krishna's closest devotees and were known for their supreme devotion to the Lord.

[37] As a child, Krishna adored butter and curd. He would innocently steal butter from the gopis and was known as the little Butter Thief.

control. It is God's will that prevails. What we can do is to strive and go forward, using the abilities God has given us. Never stop making an effort. It is essential to strive, that we try putting forth our best effort in everything we do.

Prakrti, vikrti, samskrti

Another question is how we should live this life that God has given us. *Prakrti, vikrti, samskrti* is a common saying. There are four men. Each has a piece of bread. The first man eats his bread as soon as he gets it. The second man snatches the third man's bread and eats that in addition to his own piece. The fourth man gives half of his bread to the third man who has lost his own.

The first man's behavior is *prakrti* – his nature. He thinks of his own happiness. He neither harms nor helps anyone. The second man's conduct is *vikrti* – a distortion of normal nature. He fulfills his own selfish desire even to the point of hurting others. The behavior of the fourth man is *samskrti* – true refinement. He gives to others what he has and puts the welfare of the world above his own happiness. We, too, should be able to share this life of ours for the benefit of others. This is *samskrti*, true culture, true refinement.

Some people say, "What I have amassed, I have lost; and what I gave away, I still have." What does this mean? If we give something to others, we will certainly get it back tomorrow, if not today. On the other hand, whatever we hoard out of selfishness will be lost in a little while. Whatever happens, we won't be able to take anything with us when we die. But when we give, our hearts become full, just like the hearts of those who receive from us. Amma remembers a story in this connection.

A boy used to pass by an orphanage on his way to school. He saw the unhappy faces of the orphans and it melted his heart. The Onam festival approached, and his father gave him some money. He thought, "I have my father and mother to buy me toys and new clothes. But who will make those children happy? They don't have parents. They have nobody to call their own. How sad they must be!" Suddenly, he got an idea. He went to his friends and said, "Let's pool the money we get for Onam and buy some toys and masks. We can sell those things in town, and make money that way. And with that money we can buy more things and sell those as well. With our earnings we can buy enough toys and give them to the children at the orphanage."

But the other children didn't like his idea. With their money, they wanted to buy toys for themselves. They were thinking only of their own happiness. At last, one of the boys agreed to join him. So, the two of them put their money together and bought toys and masks. They wore the masks and went to the busy intersections in town and put on a show. People burst out laughing when they saw their antics. The boys said to everyone, "Please buy some masks and toys from us and give them to your children. It will make them laugh and be happy, and you will be happy as well. You laugh when you see us play with these masks, but there are many who cannot laugh. Please help us make them laugh by buying something from us!"

The words and behavior of the boys pleased the people, and they bought their whole stock. The boys then bought more items with that money and sold them all. With the proceeds, they bought lots of toys and masks. On Onam Day, the two boys brought all the gifts over to the orphanage. When they arrived, the orphans were feeling miserable and couldn't even smile. The boys called all of them and put masks on their faces. They lit fire-blossom sticks (*poothiri*) and gave one to each child. The children forgot their sorrows. They danced with joy and ran around laughing and playing. Meanwhile, the boy who had arranged all this totally forgot to put on a mask or light a *poothiri* for himself. He watched the fun, frolic and laughter of all the others and wasn't aware of anything else. In their happiness, he completely forgot about himself, and his eyes overflowed with tears of joy. The happiness he experienced was far greater than that of all his friends. He didn't take anything for himself; but he received everything from what he gave. This is the greatness of compassion. We will get back only what we give – love if it is love, and anger if it is anger.

Look at the world, my children! So many people are suffering. Countless people are so poor that they can't afford even one meal. There are those who are in terrible pain because they can't afford to buy a single painkiller. And while all this is happening, others are squandering their money on tobacco, alcohol, and expensive clothes. If they wanted to, the ten percent of people who are wealthy in this country could uplift the poor. If they were to set their minds to it, there would no longer be any poverty in this land. In truth, the truly poor are those who have become rich by amassing for themselves the share that belongs to others. They just don't realize this.

The purpose of life is to look inward and know the Self. Only those who know the Self are truly rich. They are the ones who have real wealth. There is nothing left for them to worry about. Those who come close to them can also partake in and enjoy that wealth.

Ninety percent of all physical and mental problems arise from the pains of the past. At present we bear those wounds through life. The only way to heal those wounds is to love one another with open hearts. Just as the body needs food to grow, the soul needs love. From that love we derive the strength and vitality that we can't even get from breast milk. Let us all try to become one through mutual love! Let that be our vow!

Part two

Take refuge in Me alone

Abandoning all dharmas,
take refuge in Me alone.
I will liberate you from all sins.
Do not grieve!

— *Bhagavad Gita 18, 66*

My children,
Self-realization is the ability
to see ourselves in all living beings.

— *Sri Mata Amritanandamayi*

Surrender everything to God

My children, our minds have become stuck to material things. Our minds are full of selfishness. Because of this, there's no place within us for God to reside. The reason for going to an ashram and taking refuge in a spiritual master is to attain freedom from this condition, and to purify the mind. But, today, even in such places people pray for material wealth. They say the words, "I have great love for God" but what is needed is to surrender the things that keep the mind in bondage. Only then will our surrender and love for God become clearly known to us.

A girl wrote a letter to her friend for her birthday. "I was so happy when I thought about your birthday. I spent ages looking for a beautiful present for you. Finally, I found it in a store, but it cost ten rupees so I didn't buy it. Perhaps I'll buy it for you on another occasion." The girl loved her friend very much – she had said she would even give her life for her friend – but she was not ready to spend ten rupees for her. This is what our love and devotion for God is like. We only mouth the words, "I have surrendered everything to God."

In order to gain something, we promise a coconut to the deity at the temple. But once we get what we wished for, we look for the cheapest, smallest coconut to offer to God. My children, real love and devotion are not like this at all. We should be ready to offer even our lives. If we give something to God, it is we who benefit from it. To think otherwise is like filling a pail of water from the gutter and offering it to the river, saying, "O river, you must be thirsty! Drink this!" God doesn't want anything from us. It is God who gives us everything. God is the one who purifies us. By associating with God, we are being cleansed.

My children, only a mind with a sense of *dharma* gains proximity to God. What were the people of old like? They were prepared to sacrifice even their lives for the sake of a baby bird. It is this sense of *dharma* that brings us closer to God, the Supreme Being. It is our expansiveness of mind that qualifies us to be close to God and makes God's qualities reflect in us. Such a mind nurtures the divine qualities that are already within us. Our good actions and positive qualities are like a fertilizer that nurtures the seed, so that it can grow into a tree. God's grace will not reach a selfish mind. We have to give up our selfishness if we are to qualify for divine grace. Following the path of *dharma* is the way to achieve this. Just as we get ten seeds from sowing one seed, when we give to God we are given back a thousand fold. When we surrender ourselves to God we receive a thousandfold in return. God is the Power that protects us and not someone whom we have to protect. This has to be clearly understood.

If we cannot surrender our bodies or minds to God, can't we surrender our desires? But we first have to surrender the selfishness that is an obstacle to this.

Do you need to continue carrying your luggage after you've boarded the train? Put it down! The train will carry the load and take it to the goal. Let go of the burden. You no longer have to carry it yourself.

Having faith in God, the attitude of surrender grows in us, and we experience peace and harmony. As long as a person is selfish, he or she will have to carry the burden; God is not responsible for it. It is not enough to trust your doctor. You have to take the medicines and follow the diet restrictions that the doctor suggests. Faith in God alone is not enough. We have to live according to God's principles. This is how we are cured of the sickness of *samsara* (the endless cycle of birth, death, and rebirth) and attain our goal.

My children, place all your burdens at God's feet and live in peace and harmony!

Devotion is positive action

It is not those who just praise God, but those who live according to His principles who become qualified for God's grace. They are the ones who make gains in life.

A rich man had two assistants. One of them used to follow him around, saying, "Master! Master!" He constantly praised his master, but didn't do any work. The other assistant hardly ever went near his master. He was totally focused on completing the work assigned to him. He worked for his master, forsaking food and sleep. Which assistant did the master love?

Rama's grace flows more to those who live according to his words than to those who keep calling out, "O Rama! Rama!" God is more pleased with those who do *tapas* and selfless service. This doesn't mean that we shouldn't call out to God. But calling out to God will bring fruit only if it is accompanied by good actions. Negative actions cancel out the positive results that are gained from the chanting of the divine names, and will destroy our good *samskaras*.

People go to temples and circumambulate the deity three times, and on their way out they abuse the poor beggar standing at the door, shouting at him or her to go away. My dear children, this isn't devotion at all. Being compassionate towards the poor is our duty to God. My children, you are doing good deeds, but also bad deeds. Because of this, you lose the fruits you have gained through your positive actions. Keep a heap of sugar on one side and a large colony of ants on the other – what more do you need for the sugar to be lost? It is enough to chant the mantra a few times if it is accompanied by good actions. This is equal to chanting the mantra a whole day.

Our lives should be blessed by our good thoughts and deeds. This is not very difficult to achieve. Try to see only the good in everything. Do not feel envious of anyone. Live without unnecessary luxuries. If you are used to buying ten saris a year, begin by bringing the number down to seven, and then to five. Cut the number of unnecessary purchases this way and buy only what is needed. Spend the money you save in this way on a good cause. There are children who don't go to school because they can't afford the fees. We can help them to pay the fees. Let us at least contribute to society that much. The mantras that are chanted by people who make such contributions are what is dearest to God, because good deeds are the path that lead us to God.

You may ask, "Didn't Ajamila[38] get liberation by chanting the divine name just once?" Well, it was not actually that single utterance that brought him to God; it was the fruit of the good deeds he had done at some point in the past.

There was a merchant who spent his entire life hurting others. He hadn't performed a single good deed. Having read the story of Ajamila, he gave all his children divine names, so that he would call out their names on his deathbed and gain liberation.[39] As he drew close to death, his children gathered around him. He opened his eyes and looked at them. He saw they were all present. It worried him that all of them were there and that no one was looking after his store. "Who is in the store?" he blurted out, and with that he breathed his last. This will be the fate of anyone who goes through life without remembering God and yet hopes to gain liberation by calling out to God only at the very end. The thoughts that arise in a person's mind at the very end of life will

---

[38] Ajamila's story is told in the Shrimad Bhagavatam. He was a Brahmin who fell into bad company, married a prostitute, and led a life of corruption and cruelty. He was deeply attached to the youngest of his ten sons, whose name was Narayana, which is Lord Vishnu's name. As Ajamila lay dying and he called out his son's name, the attendants of Lord Vishnu immediately appeared and chased away the messengers of the Lord of Death who had come to take away Ajamila's soul.

[39] In Hinduism and other Eastern religions it is believed that the last thought that enters the dying person's mind will influence the nature of his or her next life.

correspond with the actions that were performed throughout his or her life. The person's actions will influence his or her final thoughts. By filling one's life with good actions, good thoughts will enter the mind at the end.

By performing selfless actions while chanting the divine names, householders achieve the same result as the sages do through their *tapas*. With meditation, the person performing *tapas* brings the mind, which normally wanders in different directions, to one point. The sages, who live according to the spiritual principles, dedicate the strength they gain from their austerities to the world. Service to the world is the path the masters prescribe for householders who cannot spend the entire day meditating and repeating a mantra. They then gain liberation by the grace of the master, whose heart melts at seeing their selfless service. A *Satguru* (realized master) is like a tortoise. Just as it is said that the tortoise hatches her eggs with the power of her thoughts, householders can gain liberation through the *Satguru's* thought. What is gained through selfless service is not in any way inferior to what is attained through *tapas*. This doesn't imply that we don't need to call out to God. It means that our prayers should be accompanied by positive actions. God won't listen to the empty chanting of His names – it has to be accompanied by our good actions. Without this, we won't receive God's compassion.

Lord Krishna encouraged Arjuna to fight. He didn't say, "I will destroy all those people and save you! You just sit here!" Instead he said, "You should fight, Arjuna! I will be with you." This shows the necessity of human effort.

The need for a spiritual master

My children, the advantage of doing *tapas* must be understood in the light of the situations we face. When we face difficult situations, we have to proceed without our minds weakening and without faltering. This is true greatness. Experiencing peace while sitting in meditation and feeling agitated when coming out of it doesn't befit a seeker. Anyone can sing without accompaniment. But the singer's skill with voice modulation in harmony with the keynote becomes evident only when singing to the accompaniment of a harmonium and keeping time. Similarly, true abidance for a seeker means keeping the rhythm and harmony of the mind, whatever the circumstance may be. This is true *tapas*. If anger arises, we shouldn't succumb to it. Yielding to anger and being enslaved by the circumstances does not befit a seeker at all.

There was an ironsmith in a village in the Himalayan foothills. He would bend metal rods by beating them on a stone near his workshop. One day as he approached the stone, he came across a cobra. It lay there the next day as well, unable to move because of the cold. The ironsmith prodded the snake, but it didn't stir. Feeling pity for it, he carried it into his workshop and gave it milk and fruits. He returned to work. He heated an iron rod in the fire and beat it into shape, and as he brought it out, it touched the snake. The cobra raised its hood, ready to strike him. He had thought that the snake was very docile, that it wouldn't hurt anyone. But when exposed to the heat in the smithy, it wasn't cold any longer, and its nature changed. Likewise, when one performs *tapas*, the mind is 'frozen' – but if one isn't careful, the innate tendencies will rise up again the moment the environment becomes conducive for them. The spiritual aspirant should therefore strengthen the mind, so that he or she can face and transcend any situation without faltering. The spiritual master's task is to raise the disciple to that level. In each situation, our mind should see everything as God, as the Self. Only then can we say that we are strong.

We should train our minds to see only the good, the divine principle, in everything, and savor the bliss of the Self like the bee that searches for honey in the flowers and tastes only honey. If there is anger or ego hiding anywhere within the disciple, it is

143

the master's duty to expose it and eradicate it. The maturity the disciple gains by being in the master's presence for a short span of time would not be attainable through a long period of spiritual practice alone. When giving any work to the disciple, however easy or difficult the task, the master's aim is to eliminate the disciple's ego and make him or her fit for the realization of the Self. What the disciple needs is a certificate from the master. It is the duty of the disciple to obey the master's every word. Like the hammer in the hand of the blacksmith, the disciple should become a tool in the master's hands. The disciple should accept every command of the master. The master has absolute authority and command over the disciple. Only when the disciple allows him- or herself to become an instrument, will there be progress.

A young student failed four or five times in every class before passing. Finally, he somehow managed to reach the tenth grade, the highest class in the school. The boy was convinced he wouldn't pass even if he took the tenth grade examination ten times. But his class teacher decided that he would help the boy to pass that year. Day and night, without rest, he taught the boy all the lessons. He took special care to see that the boy's attention didn't wander from his studies. Finally, the time came for the exam. The boy took the exam and passed at the first attempt. The *Satguru* is like that teacher, who brought success to a student whom everyone else had written off as incapable of succeeding. It is very difficult to attain the world of the Self, even if we try for a thousand lifetimes. However, with the master's help, the disciple can attain enlightenment in just one life.

Being permitted to live with the master doesn't mean that one is accepted as a disciple. The master accepts a person as a disciple only after observing and testing him or her thoroughly. A real disciple has complete faith in every word of the master, and responds to those words with attentive awareness. The disciple also has the attitude of surrender to the master.

Only through renunciation can immortality be attained

My children, we have often heard the mantra, *Tyagenaike amritatvamanashuh* (Only through renunciation can one attain immortality). This is not a mantra only to be chanted or listened to; it is a principle to be emulated in life. More than chanted, it has to be lived.

If our baby falls ill, we'll carry that baby to the hospital; and if we can't find a vehicle, we'll walk, even if the hospital is far away. We are ready to fall at the feet of any number of people to get our baby admitted. If no private room is available, the parents, however high and mighty they are, will be ready to spend the night in the general ward, even sleeping on the filthy floor. They will take leave from their work for days on end to watch over their child. But all this is done for their own baby, and for their own peace of mind. So, it cannot be called real renunciation or sacrifice.

We are ready to climb up and down the steps of judicial courts many times for a cent of land, but we do this for the sake of our own property. We give up sleep and work overtime at night, but it is done to earn more money for ourselves. None of this can be called renunciation.

Renunciation is to disregard one's own comfort and happiness while helping others. If we spend our hard-earned money for the sake of a suffering fellow human being, it is renunciation. When the neighbor's child is sick at the hospital and there is no one to help, and we volunteer to spend nights at the hospital watching over the child, [40] without expecting anything in return, not even

---

[40] Unlike at western hospitals, at Indian hospitals, nurses provide only medical treatment. An inpatient therefore has a relative or friend staying with him or her at the hospital, to buy medicine and to help with the patient's personal needs.

a smile from anyone, that is renunciation. If we take the money we save by foregoing some of our own comforts and use it for a good cause, that can also be called renunciation.

Through such actions, we are knocking at the door to the world of the Self, and our selfless actions open that door for us. Only such actions qualify as *karma yoga* (the path of selfless action). Selfless actions lead the individual soul to the world of the Self, while other actions lead to death. No action performed with the attitude of 'I' and 'mine' will ever come to our aid.

We visit a friend whom we haven't seen for a long time, and we lovingly give that person a bouquet of flowers. But we are the ones who first enjoy the beauty and fragrance of the bouquet, and experience the satisfaction of giving it away. Similarly, we experience joy and satisfaction when we act selflessly.

There is an aura around our bodies, and just as our voice is recorded on a tape, all of our actions leave their imprints on the aura. When one's actions are selfless, the aura becomes golden in color. All obstacles disappear from the paths of such people, regardless of what they set out to do. Everything is auspicious for them. When they die, they dissolve into the bliss of the Supreme Being, the Absolute Reality, just as the gas in a soda bottle merges into the atmosphere when the bottle breaks. On the other hand, the aura of those who perform negative actions becomes dark, and they will never be free of problems and hurdles. When they die, their aura stays down on the earthly plane and becomes food for bugs and insects. And they will have to be born here again.

My children, even if someone who performs selfless actions doesn't find the time to repeat or chant a mantra, he or she will attain immortality. Like nectar, such a person is beneficial to others. A selfless life is the greatest spiritual discourse anyone can give. Others can see and emulate it.

Charity

My children, if we don't have awareness and discrimination when we give charity, we will have to suffer because of the actions of those who receive our gifts. If a healthy man comes up begging, don't give him any money. You can give him food, though. Tell him to work for a living. By giving healthy people money, we make them lazy. They may use the money on alcohol and drugs; they may be doing many negative things. By giving them money, we give them the opportunity to do those negative things, and, we, too, will have to bear the fruits. If such people ask for money, offer to pay them to work. You can offer them some work in your yard or any kind of work. Pay them only after the work is done. Find out whether the person is willing to do this. People who are unwilling to do any work are destructive. To help someone like that is to create a lazy person, and we are thus harming the world. If we feed someone for nothing, he or she will just sit doing nothing, get sick due to lack of exercise, and become a burden to him- or herself and the world. The largest gathering of lazy people can be observed in front of charitable places where free food is distributed.

But we can help the poor who cannot work because of ill health. We can help orphans who cannot afford an education. We can help those children by paying their school fees and other expenses. We should help widows who are struggling because they have no means to survive. We can aid those who have lost their limbs and cannot even go begging for food. We can buy medicine for the destitute who are sick and can't afford to buy medicine. We can donate money to ashrams and other institutions that have service projects, but we should first find out if they are actually spending that money on serving the poor and the suffering. Ashrams and such institutions can provide services that benefit society in general, so by helping them we are helping society as a whole. We therefore need to exercise great care and discrimination when we give in charity. Our kindness and the help we give should never lead to the recipient's wrongdoing. Regardless of who we are helping, we should never expect any kindness in return. Sometimes, we may receive abuse in return. Having any expectation that someone will be kind to us in return will only cause us sorrow. Our mind should be like an incense stick that burns out while giving its fragrance to everyone, even to the one who burns it. This is what brings us to the feet of Supreme Being. We should be of benefit even to those who harm us. Our minds should have the attitude of offering flowers in return for the thorns that are thrown at us. By developing our minds in this way, we can live in peace and harmony.

Laugh wholeheartedly

My children, is there anyone amongst us who doesn't like to laugh? Of course not. If there are some who don't laugh, it is because of the pain and sadness that fill their hearts. Once that suffering disappears, they will automatically laugh. But, nowadays, how many of us are able to laugh wholeheartedly? We break into a smile when we crack jokes or see our friends, but at the same time there is an ache within us. A true smile originates in the heart. Only a genuine smile lights up our faces and the hearts of those around us.

Many people's laughter has become no more than the expansion and contraction of certain facial muscles. There is no purity of heart in such laughter. Laughing at the mistakes committed by others isn't real laughter. We should be able to burst out laughing at our own mistakes. We should be able to laugh deeply, forgetting everything – remembering only the Supreme Truth. That is true laughter, the laughter of bliss. But are we able to do this?

Today, we laugh mostly when we recall the defects of others or are saying negative things about others. My children, speaking badly of others is to malign ourselves.

Amma remembers a story. A master had two disciples. Both of them were equally egoistic, and they always criticized each other. Their behavior didn't change, no matter how much the master counseled them. Finally the master found a solution. One night, as both of the disciples were fast asleep, he painted their faces in bright colors to make them look like clowns. When one of them woke up in the morning and saw the other man's face, he started laughing loudly. "Ha ha ha!" he guffawed. Hearing this, the second disciple also got up. The moment he caught sight of the other's man's face, he, too, burst out laughing, and they were both roaring with laughter. While this was going on, someone brought a mirror, held it up in front of one of the disciples, and said, "Look!" The disciple snatched the mirror, held it in front of the other disciple's face, and said, "Look at this!" With that, the laughter quickly drained away from both of them. My children, that's what we ourselves are like. We speak ill of others, without realizing that they, too, are making fun of our mistakes.

It is easy, my children, to find fault with others and to laugh at them, but we shouldn't do that. We should discover our own faults and mistakes and laugh at them instead. This will elevate us.

Now, about happiness: there are two ways in which we can obtain happiness. We rejoice when something good happens to us, or we rejoice at the misfortune of others. Sorrow also comes in two ways: there is our own sorrow, and the happiness of others is also our sorrow.

A businessman sent a ship abroad, loaded with merchandise. But the ship sank. The businessman was so overwhelmed with grief that he became bedridden. He no longer ate, slept, or spoke. He constantly brooded over his loss. He was treated by many doctors and psychiatrists, but his grief and illness did not abate. He just continued to lie there. Then one day his son came running in and said, "Father, did you hear the news? That man who always challenged you, his company building caught fire! Nothing is left – he lost everything!" The instant he heard this, the man who had been lying there silently for so long, suddenly jumped up and burst out laughing. He said, "That's great! I always thought something like that should happen to him because of his ego! Son, bring me something to eat! Quick!" Here was someone who hadn't been able to eat or sleep until that moment; and, yet, he was suddenly overjoyed when he heard that someone else had lost everything.

My children, this is the nature of our happiness. At present, our laughter depends on the sorrow of others. That is not true laughter. We should grieve with others when they grieve, and rejoice with them when they are happy. We should see everyone as part of our own Self. Only when our hearts become pure because of our love and selflessness will we begin to enjoy the bliss that is our true nature. Only then can we laugh fully. Until then, our laughter is a mere act, because we do not experience any true joy from it.

Love without attachment and serve without expectation

My darling children, many of you may wonder why the ashram runs a hospital. Didn't the Lord incarnate as Dhanvantari (the Lord of medicine)? Didn't he show us that medicines and medical treatment are essential? The scriptures say we have to maintain the body. If we examine the lives of the great souls of the past we can see how true this is. Sri Ramakrishna, Swami Vivekananda, Ramana Maharshi – all of them underwent treatment when they fell ill. They didn't sit quietly without treatment, declaring, "I am Brahman (the Absolute Reality) and not the body." Because disease is the nature of the body, it is essential to undergo treatment and maintain the body. Only if there is fuel, can there be fire. Similarly, if we are to know the Self, it is necessary to sustain our instrument. Spirituality is not incompatible with hospitals or medical treatment. On the contrary, such things help to sustain the body, which is the instrument we use to know the Self.

There are many people who have come to stay at the ashram after having met Amma. They have come from India and abroad. Many of them are doctors. They wish to be with Amma. So Amma thought she'd give them the opportunity to do *seva* (selfless service) by doing the work they are familiar with – because how many people can meditate for twenty four hours a day? So what will they do during the rest of the time when they are not meditating? If they just sit around doing nothing, many kinds of thoughts will arise. That is also action, and is of no use to anyone. But if they do something practical, it will benefit the world.

Some may say they want only liberation and nothing else, not even medical treatment that may be necessary, and that they are ready to die of illness if it comes to that. But they also need God's grace to get liberation, and to receive that grace, they have to have internal purity. To develop this purity, selfless actions are required. It is through selfless actions that one becomes qualified to receive God's grace. And to do selfless actions, it is necessary to sustain the body by treating any illnesses.

Jnana (supreme knowledge) and *bhakti* (devotion) are like the two sides of a coin, and *karma* (action) is the engraving on that coin. It is the engraving that gives the coin its value.

Bhakti and *karma* can be described as the two wings of a bird, while *jnana* is its tail. Only with all three can the bird soar to great heights.

Even in the *gurukulas* of old, the disciples worked. They didn't think of it as *karma*. To them, it was *guru seva*, service to the spiritual master. An action performed for the spiritual master is not action; it is meditation. It is said that one should do *seva* with the attitude that the ashram is the master's body. Later, one should see the entire world as the master's body and serve it. This is real meditation. Indeed, to constantly remember this principle is also meditation.

Most people know the story of the disciple[41] who lay down in front of the broken embankment to stop flood waters from inundating his master's field. To the disciple, that field was not a mere field. He was willing to surrender even his body to prevent the destruction of the master's crops. This cannot be called mere action. The state in which one totally forgets oneself, this is the highest state of meditation. In the olden days, all the work in the *gurukula* was done by the disciples. They collected firewood from the forest, grazed the cows, and did other chores. They didn't think of this as mere work. For them, it was spiritual practice; it was service to the master and a form of meditation.

Hundreds of Amma's children who are educated and have work experience come here. How can they start meditating all day as soon as they arrive here? Doing some work that benefits the world is so much better than sitting without being able to meditate properly and allowing the mind to be polluted by more and more thoughts. Everyone can perform actions that are suited to their abilities while chanting a mantra. This will benefit them as well as the world. It creates internal purity, and brings us closer to the goal.

No one can reach the goal without effort. Effort is indispensable in both worldly and spiritual life. However, it is divine grace that brings completion to the effort and gives it beauty, and a selfless attitude is what qualifies one for that grace.

---

[41] A story from the epic, Mahabharata. The disciple was Aruni, who, through his spiritual master's blessing, became a great sage.

My children, when you perform selfless service for the world, you may think, "Because of all this work, I don't get even a moment to think of God. All my time is lost in work. Is my life going to be useless?" But those who perform selfless actions don't have to tire themselves looking for God anywhere, because God's true shrine is the heart of the person who does selfless service.

This is how each of the institutions here has grown. When Amma's children who were experienced in the field of education arrived, they started schools. Computer experts came and joined, and they started computer institutions. My children who are engineers arrived and they set out to construct the buildings needed for the institutions. Doctors came, and they became instrumental in starting the hospitals. To them, none of this is work; it is spiritual practice, meditation, and *guru seva*. My children, Amma will tell you that it is beneficial just to be exposed to the breath of those who, forgetting themselves, work for the good of the world.

Some followers of the path of Vedanta say that an action creates new tendencies, even if it is performed for the benefit of the world. But those are the statements of lazy people. In the Gita, Lord Krishna says, "Arjuna, I have nothing to be gained in all the three worlds. Yet I keep performing actions."

Perform your actions without attachment. Act without the attitude, "I am doing." Act instead with the attitude, "God is making me do this." Such work can never cause bondage, but will lead to liberation. In any section of the Gita you can see that it is human effort that is given importance.

Even the Vedantins[42] who say, "I am Brahman, so why should I do any work?" go for treatment when they get ill. They demand to be given their lunch at precisely one o'clock, and their beds have to be made by ten in the evening. If they need all this service, why doesn't it occur to them that the world also needs help? If

---

[42] Those who follow the path of Vedanta.

one holds the view that everything is identical with the one Self, then, nothing can be rejected; everything has to be accepted. You can gauge the spiritual attitude of someone by observing his or her degree of selflessness.

There are those who think that all a *sannyasi* needs to do is go to the Himalayas and live there. My children, selfless service to the world is the beginning of the real quest for the Self. It is also the end of that quest. Our duty to God is to be compassionate towards those who are suffering and in need. Our highest, most important duty in this world is to help our fellow beings. God doesn't need anything from us. The Supreme Being is always complete. The sun doesn't need candlelight. God is the Protector of the entire universe. God is the personification of love and compassion. We become expansive only by imbibing that love and compassion. *Sannyasis* learn to love without any attachment, and to serve without any expectation. They have to discard the baggage of selfishness and lift onto their shoulders the burden of service to the world.

We become eligible for God's grace only when we are able to love and serve all living beings without any selfish desires. To meditate without attaining internal purity through selfless service is as wasteful as pouring milk into a dirty vessel. We forget this truth. We forget our obligation to serve those who are struggling. We visit the temple and perform worship, but when we come out of that place and are confronted by those who are sick or unable to find work, and they extend their hands towards us for a little food, we ignore them or shout at them and drive them away. My children, true worship of God is the loving kindness we show the suffering.

So, my children, we should go out amidst those who are suffering. But along with our service activities, we should also try to impart some of the spiritual principles to people. Giving the hungry food is important, but not enough. Even if we fill their stomachs, their hunger will return again after a little while. We should also explain the spiritual principles to them. We should make them understand the purpose of life and the nature of the world. Then they will learn to be happy and contented under any circumstance. Only then will our service be completely fruitful.

Today, everyone aims at a higher status in life than their own. No one bothers to think of the condition of those who are less fortunate than themselves.

Amma remembers a story. There was a poor widow who worked as a servant in the home of a rich man. Her only daughter was physically challenged. The woman would bring the girl along when she went to work. The rich man also had a daughter. The daughter was very fond of the servant's child. She would caress the little girl, feed her sweets, and tell her stories. But her father didn't like this. Day after day he scolded his daughter, saying, "You shouldn't play with her! Why are you carrying that dirty, crippled child around?" His daughter didn't reply. He thought perhaps she was playing with the child because she had no one else to play with. So, one day he brought home the daughter of one of his friends. His daughter saw the girl, smiled, talked to her in a friendly way, and then picked up the servant's child and began expressing affection towards her. Seeing this, her father asked, "Darling, don't you like this girl Daddy brought to play with you?" She replied, "I like her very much, but I would like to say something. Even if I didn't like the girl you brought here, she would have so many others to love her. But, Dad, with this other child, if I don't love her, who else will love her? She has no friends of her own."

My children, this should be our attitude. You should whole-heartedly love the poor and the suffering. Emphasize with them and uplift them. This is our duty to God.

You may ask, "If selfless service is so great, what is the need for meditation and *tapas*?" My children, if an ordinary person is like an electric post, a person who does *tapas* is like a transformer. It is possible to gain great power through *tapas*. It is like generating power by building a dam across a river that flows through nine channels. But we should also be willing to dedicate the power we gain through *tapas* to the welfare of the world. We should be ready to offer everything, like an incense stick that burns itself out while spreading fragrance everywhere. God's grace flows automatically to those whose hearts are that expansive.

My children, we should try to develop compassion. We should feel an urgency to serve the suffering. We should be ready to work for the welfare of the world in every situation.

Many people meditate by just shutting their eyes, or by trying only to open a third eye and go beyond the two eyes that see the world. They will not succeed. Sitting in meditation is very important, but it is not enough. We cannot shut our eyes to the world in the name of spirituality. To be able to see our own Self in every living thing with our eyes open – this is Self-realization. We have to see ourselves in others, and love and serve them. This is how spiritual practice attains perfection.

Part three

With His hands and feet everywhere

With His hands and feet everywhere,
with His eyes, heads, and ears on all sides,
He dwells in the world, enveloping all.

- Bhagavad Gita 13, 14

My children,
only if we can create people who have
the strength and vitality of the Self,
and an attitude of self-surrender,
will this country develop and prosper.

- Sri Mata Amritanandamayi

Amma speaking to het children during an Onam celebration

Universal Love – the fulfillment of devotion

Amma's message at the celebration of Onam in Amritapuri

The festival of Onam is a day when we are reminded of the devotee merging with the Supreme Being. Only if we completely surrender our minds to God can we merge into His feet.

But how do we surrender our minds? When we surrender that which our mind is most attached to, it is equal to surrendering the mind. Today, our minds are most strongly attached to our wealth. We are not ready to give up even the smallest thing. If we go on a spiritual pilgrimage, we keep some cash on hand to give to beggars. But, as far as possible, we will have collected one- or two-*paisa*[43] coins, certainly not anything of a higher denomination than five paisa. The aim of charity is to turn our selfish minds into unselfish ones, and, at the same time, to give the poor what they need. But we are miserly even in this. We are stingy even when making an offering to the deity at the temple. Real surrender to God lies not in words alone, but in our actions. The sincere devotee is he or she who has total surrender to God. Today, we don't even have the right to utter the word 'devotee.' But Mahabali was different. He surrendered to God everything he had. As a result, there was no delay in his attaining the supreme state. It is often said that the Lord pushed Mahabali with His foot down to Patala, the netherworld. But this is not true. The Lord made Mahabali's soul merge into Himself. And the body, which was the product of ignorance, was sent to the world it deserved.

Even though Mahabali was born into a lineage of *asuras*,[44] he was a devotee who possessed many good qualities. But he was also

---

[43] A paisa is one hundredth of a rupee.

[44] A demon or a person with demonic qualities.

very proud and thought, "I am the King! I am wealthy enough to give away anything as a gift." He didn't realize that because of his pride, he was losing everything he should have gained. Although he was generous by nature, his pride hindered him from reaping the proper benefit of his being generous.

It is the duty of the Lord to remove the devotee's ego. The Lord approached Mahabali in the form of Vamana, the Divine Dwarf-Boy.[45] He asked Mahabali for just the amount of land that he could cover with three footsteps. Mahabali thought that was a very insignificant amount of land the Lord requested of the king, who had the power to give away a whole kingdom. But by the time Vamana had taken two paces, everything Mahabali owned was gone, because the entire kingdom was traversed by those two enormous footsteps. And with that, Mahabali's ego also disappeared. "How insignificant all of my wealth is before the Lord! Beside him, I am nothing!" This humility grew in him. "I have no ability. All powers are his!" With his pride gone, Mahabali bowed down in front of the Lord. He merged completely with the Supreme Spirit. In fact, as his sense of 'I' and 'mine' was destroyed by the Lord's grace, he merged at the Lord's feet. So, the Lord didn't push Mahabali down to the underworld with His foot, as is often pictured.

In the end, the Lord asked Mahabali, "Do you have any wishes?" Mahabali replied, "I have only one wish – that everyone in this world, young and old, should be able to eat their fill, wear new clothes, and dance together in joy; that this should be a world of joy and peace." This is the aspiration of a real devotee. The devotee doesn't wish for Self-realization or liberation. His or her only desire is that every living being in this world should be happy. When you turn to the path of God, some people will complain that you have forsaken everyone for the sake of your

---

[45] In incarnation of Lord Vishnu.

own liberation or for heaven. "Isn't that selfish?" they say. But the devotee takes refuge in God only so that he or she may love and serve the world selflessly. This is why a devotee performs austerities. His or her aspiration is to see a world where everyone finds joy in chanting the divine names.

Today is the day of full surrender. As long as the sense of 'I' remains, one cannot merge into the supreme state. Our selfishness has to disappear completely.

Amma remembers a story. In the ancient kingdom of Magadha, there lived a king called Jayadeva. He had three sons. As he grew old, the king decided to renounce the throne and enter the life of a *vanaprastha*. Normally, the eldest son would inherit the throne, but King Jayadeva decided to give the throne to the son who really loved the people selflessly. He called his three sons and asked, "Have you done any good deeds lately?"

The eldest son said, "Yes, I've done a good deed. A friend entrusted some gems to me for safekeeping. When he asked me for them later, I returned them all to him."

"So what?" said the king.

"I could have stolen a few gems from the collection," said the prince.

"But then, why didn't you steal?"

"If I had stolen anything, my conscience would have pricked me for doing such a thing, and that would have caused me sorrow."

"So, it was to avoid sorrow that you refrained from stealing," said the king.

He called the second prince and asked, "Have you performed any good action?"

"Yes. I was traveling when I happened to see a child being swept away in a fast-flowing river. He was about to drown and the river was full of crocodiles. Even though there were many people around, no one came forward to save him because they were afraid of the crocodiles. But I jumped into the river and saved the boy!"

"Why were you ready to sacrifice your own life to save him?" the king asked.

"If I hadn't done that, the people would have said I ran away from there out of fear even though I was the son of the king. They would have called me a coward!"

"So, you saved him to earn people's praise and for the sake of your reputation," said the king.

He called his third son and asked, "Have you performed any good action?"

"I'm not aware of having done any good deed," said the youngest prince.

The king was worried when he heard this. Not believing his son's answer, he called his subjects, and asked, "Do you know of any good deed done by my youngest son?"

Each of them said, "He always enquires about our comfort and happiness. He gives us money when we need it and helps us; when we starve, he sends us food; he builds houses for the homeless. The good deeds he has done are endless, but he has specifically instructed us not to tell anyone about his actions."

King Jayadeva realized that his youngest son was the best of his sons, and he gave him the throne.

My children, whatever you do, the attitude "*I* am doing this" should not be present. Don't do things just to impress others. Look upon each action as a way of worshipping God. It is only because of God's power that we are able to do anything. The well says, "People drink from my water, and it is thanks to me that they can bathe and wash!" But the well doesn't consider where its water comes from.

My children, we are just instruments. Everything is due to God's power. Do not forget this! Surrender yourselves completely to God as you proceed in life. God will protect you.

My children, our love and attachment should be directed to the Supreme Being. All those whom we now call our own, our kith and kin, are bound to leave us if the circumstances change even slightly. The Supreme Being is our true relative. The Supreme Being alone is eternal. We should be aware of this at all times. Then we won't have to grieve.

"O Mother, if I hold your hand, I may let go and run after some toy I see! At times I may fall into the pits that are the joys and sorrows of this world. But if you hold my hand, that will not happen, for you are with me always. I am safe in your hands." Pray like this, my children. Take care not to stop thinking about God. Surrender yourself fully to Him! Then you will definitely be able to reach the supreme state.

Amrita Kripa Sagar, the hospice for terminally ill cancer patients in Mumbai

Compassion – the core of spirituality

Amma's benedictory address on the occasion of laying the foundation stone for Amrita Kripa Sagar, the hospice in Mumbai for terminally ill cancer patients, which Amma's organization, the M.A. Math, opened in 1995.

My children, what we need is not discourses, but action. By now, Amma has traveled in most regions of the world. She has had a chance to meet hundreds of thousands of people, and has witnessed the pain they have suffered. This is why Amma decided to establish something like this.

Love is what is lacking the most in today's world. Many couples come to Amma for *darshan*. The wife says, "Amma, my husband doesn't love me!" If Amma asks the husband, "Son, why don't you love her?" the answer usually is, "But I *do* love her! I just don't show it, that's all!"

My children, that is not enough. What is the use of honey that is locked inside a stone? What is the use of giving ice to someone who is dying of thirst? That is what it's like when you say, "I have love for her within me." Your love should be clearly expressed, my children!

Without the passport of love, we cannot get the visa needed for liberation. The scriptures say we should wish that the world receives from us what we ourselves desire to get from the world. We want others to give us joy, and, therefore, we should never give sorrow to others. Christ says you should love your neighbor just as you love yourself. The Koran says that if your enemy's donkey is sick, you should treat it. But, nowadays, our way of thinking is different. Life has changed completely. There is no more compassion. We are gladdened if the neighboring shop loses its business or if the neighbors are unhappy. And if they are happy we feel unhappy. This is the compassion that is felt for others!

My children, if you have true love, that itself is the Truth. True love is God. It is *dharma*. It is bliss.

When there is true love, one cannot tell a lie, because then there is only room for Truth. We do not harm those whom we truly love. In that state all violence ends. Where there is true love, all dualities disappear. In a flooded field, the embankments form the boundaries. If those embankments are removed, there will be only one body of water. In love, all distinctions automatically disappear. In love, everything is contained.

Some may interpret love differently, and that is fine. The man who goes to the field to find food for his cows sees grass there, while the herbalist sees medicinal plants in the same field. People have different natures, and things can be interpreted differently. But this is Amma's path.

The abundant river doesn't need any water. On the other hand, we need pure river water in order to clean our gutters. God doesn't want anything from us. Around us, so many people are suffering. Let us console them. Let us give them the aid they need. This is true love for God. This is the real spiritual principle.

Many of Amma's children have come to her weeping bitterly. One day she asked a weeping boy, "What happened, son?" He said, "My mother has cancer, and yesterday she cried for eight hours because she was in so much pain, and we couldn't afford to buy her any painkillers!"

Imagine that woman having to cry aloud in pain for eight hours because her family didn't have the ten or twenty rupees the pills would cost! Amma knows countless people like that. Amma decided that very day that she would do something to help those people. And that is why this hospice is being built.

When thinking of the pain of those people, something else comes to mind. When a man or a woman in an apartment cries because he or she is suffering unbearable pain, you will often find in the adjoining apartment people who are completely drunk and are smashing up everything. If they were to feel a little compassion for those who are crying in pain, their selfishness would vanish.

Those who are compassionate will experience the compassion of God, who is the Supreme Principle, and they will revel in the bliss of their own Self. The heroes are those who find joy within themselves. That is a sign of courage. Those who depend on other objects for their joy are not courageous; they are weak.

The doctors stop treating a cancer patient when nothing more can be done for that person. Realizing that the doctors can no longer help, the patient's family begins to hate the doctors, and they forsake the dying person. Having lost all support, he or she lies dying little by little, awaiting death at any moment, bearing the bodily pain as well as the mental anguish caused by the family's rejection. We can see such people on the streets of Mumbai.

We all want opportunities to do spiritual practice and selfless service. Let us then help and console those who live in pain, and also talk to them about spiritual values. This is Amma's hope. Many people who are sick have lost all hope. The help we give them is true service.

My children, prayer is not just chanting a mantra. A kind word, a smiling face, compassion – this is all part of prayer. Without loving kindness, no matter how much *tapas* we do, it is like pouring milk into a dirty vessel.

Some people ask, "What is more important, spiritual practice or action?" True *tapas* is maintaining the balance of both body and mind under all circumstances. Some people are good at spiritual practice but flare up in anger for minor reasons. When this happens, they have no idea what they are saying or doing.

There are others who perform actions with great sincerity and enthusiasm, but collapse when faced with insignificant problems, completely losing control of their minds. So, focusing on just one of them – spiritual practice or action – is not enough. We need both together. A normal person is like a candle, but he or she can shine like the sun by doing *tapas*. However, in Amma's eyes, the true *tapasvi* is one who dedicates his or her *tapas* to the world as well.

May this undertaking receive the blessings of all of you. This is Amma's prayer.

Real wealth is Love

Amma's Onam message 1995

My children, this is the day of unity and mutual dedication. By this alone can we gain true happiness. Today is the day to savor true joy. This is why people used to say, "Feast during Onam, even if you have to sell your land!" There is a great principle hidden behind this. We are interested in amassing everything in life. We hoard – even to the point of giving up food and sleep for the sake of our hoarding. We compete with each other, with little love for family or friends. We think only of work and money. But nothing of what we amass can come with us in the end. If we look at those who lead selfish lives, we can see that they actually live in hell – and hell is also where they reach after death. My children, the one thing that stands above all else and lasts forever has nothing to do with wealth, power, title, or position. It is love.

A married couple was having a conversation. The husband said, "I am going to start a big business. We'll be very wealthy in the future." The wife said, "But aren't we rich now?"

"What do you mean? What we have is barely enough to make our ends meet."

"My dear one, aren't you with me, and am I not here with you? So, what is it that we lack?" Hearing her loving words, the husband shed tears of love and embraced her. My children, love is real wealth. Love is true life.

Today, no matter how wealthy people are, they live in hell, because there is no mutual love. Only selfishness flourishes among them. This doesn't mean we shouldn't try to acquire wealth or that wealth isn't needed. But we should understand that nothing will be with us forever; nothing will accompany us. If we have this understanding, we won't be overjoyed when we acquire wealth, or sink into lasting sorrow when we lose it. Even if we lose our worldly wealth, our never-ending wealth of love will survive, imparting peace and harmony to our lives.

Thinking of Onam, many people express the opinion that injustice was done to Mahabali. "Didn't the Lord push Mahabali down into the netherworld with His foot, even though Mahabali had surrendered everything to Him?" they ask. It is true that Mahabali surrendered everything material, but with every action he did, he had the attitude, "*I* am doing this." He wouldn't give that up. That 'I' was the gift that the Lord was asking for. It is God's duty to protect His devotees. It is often said that the ego resides in the head. When we lower our heads before someone, we lose our ego. This attitude doesn't come easily to anyone. By bowing down in front of the Lord, Mahabali was in fact forsaking his body-consciousness, and entering the world of the Self. This is the ideal to be learned from that story.

A rich man had the desire to become a *sannyasi*. He gave away all of his wealth. He erected a small hut on top of a hill and moved in there. Hearing that a new *sannyasi* was living on the hill, many people came to see him. And all he had to say was, "Do you know who I am? Do you know how much wealth I had? All that you see over there was mine! I gave it all away to various people." He gave everything away and left, but none of it left his mind!

This was also the case with Mahabali. But it is the Lord's duty to save the devotee. What stood in the way of that broad-minded, generous devotee's progress towards the goal was his sense of 'I' – his ego. Humility and winning the grace of the *mahatmas* (great souls) are indispensable for eradicating the ego.

My children, whatever story you choose, the basic message is love alone. Love one another! Love with open hearts! Love each other without any expectations. Then there is no need to go anywhere in search of a true heaven.

The spiritual practice of love

There was an ashram where a spiritual master lived with his disciples. After the master left his body, the disciples lived together harmoniously for a while. Slowly, however, their spiritual practices slackened. They stopped meditating and chanting their mantras. Mutual spite and jealousy grew. Everyone's aim became position and status. The very atmosphere of the ashram changed. Fewer and fewer people visited the ashram. There was only silence there. When people become enamored with power and prestige, they go crazy. Then there are no longer any rules regarding what should or should not be done. But one of the disciples felt very sad about the state of the ashram. He visited an aged saint who lived nearby, and explained the situation to him. He described how the ashram, where hundreds of people used to visit daily and where there had always been a joyful atmosphere, was now like a cemetery.

The saint listened and said, "There is a saint amongst you. But he disguises his true state. If you follow his words, your ashram will rise to even greater heights than before, and its fame will spread." The disciple asked, "Who is it?"

But the saint had already slipped into the state of *samadhi*.[46] The disciple returned to the ashram with the news, and he pondered deeply what he had learned. "Who is the saint amongst us?" he said to a fellow disciple. "Is it the cook? Not likely. He can't even cook properly! Because of him, it's been a long time since we've enjoyed anything we've eaten. How can he be a saint? Could it be the gardener? No – he doesn't pay attention to anything. He is very impulsive. What about the man who tends the

---

[46] An inner state of perfect oneness with the Supreme Spirit, the Absolute Reality, in which the experiencer, the experience, and that which is experienced are one.

cows? Not likely. He has a terrible temper." He went on thinking like this about everyone. The other disciple said, "Why criticize their actions? One cannot evaluate the saints on the basis of their actions. Their actions are designed for our future welfare. We have to be humble towards them to benefit from them, don't we? So we shouldn't find fault in them. Let us do one thing. Let us be humble towards everyone here at the ashram. Let us try to love the others without finding fault in them. Let us observe the ashram discipline the way we used to." So they both tried to love everyone and they were polite and humble in their behavior. When the others saw this, they, too, started behaving in that way. Everyone started feeling happy, and the ashram regained its former festive air. It became an even more auspicious place than before. And all the ashram residents became eligible for Self-realization.

My children, love is the foundation of everything. Compassion towards others is the same as surrendering to God.

My children, God is within us, but today that inner presence exists only in a dormant form. For that seed to sprout, the water of compassion is needed. With the liquid of selfishness, it will only perish – that is certain. Doing something for others and not for oneself alone can be called compassion. Only in the water from that spring can the seed grow.

Meditation alone is not enough, my children. Compassion is also essential. Clothes can be washed with soap, but to remove the stains, something stronger is needed. Likewise, we need compassion along with meditation. We must have the love and empathy in our hearts that is needed to aid the suffering. This is true service. God's grace will flow only into a heart that has this compassion.

Internal spiritual practice

Amma always says that meditation is as valuable as gold. Meditation is ideal for both spiritual and material progress. The currency of a specific country is accepted only within that country; it has no value in any other country. Even within its own country a currency note won't have any value if its serial number is missing. But a gold coin is different. Even if the engraving on the coin is missing, it will still be valuable in any country. This is what meditation is like. The time spent in meditation can never be a loss. Think of how valuable gold would be if it also had a wonderful fragrance! That is what it is like when we meditate and also have compassion. Then, all the obstacles in the path of God's grace flowing towards us will disappear.

Many people come here and complain, "That person put an evil spell on me! They practiced some sorcery against me," and so on. Don't believe in any such thing, my children! What we are experiencing now are the fruits of our previous actions. It is useless to blame anyone else for this.

Life is filled with both happiness and sadness. In order to balance this and move forward, we have to understand spirituality. So-called fate is the fruit of our previous actions, and this means that our actions have great importance. So, instead of wasting your money on sorcery and such things, try to pray with concentration and give charity to those who deserve it. Such good actions will certainly bring the desired results.

Only those who have done intense *tapas* can demonstrate the power of mantras. Such people could actually harm us with certain mantras. Just as there are good mantras, there are also evil mantras. But these days, who is able to develop such powers from doing *tapas*? So, there's no need to be afraid of such things. Depending on the time of our birth, we have to undergo suffering at some stages of life. When it is very hot, we can't do anything with concentration. A person who is drunk doesn't know what he is saying and may get beaten by others because of his words. Similarly, there are difficult periods in life that depend on the time of birth. We attribute those periods to the effects of Mars, Saturn, Rahu, and so on. Loss of wealth, accidents, quarrels, diseases, the suffering of family and friends, obstacles in general, blame for mistakes that we didn't commit – all this can happen during those stages. Such events are not the results of somebody's sorcery or black magic. With the money you spend in the name of such things, you could pay off your debts instead.

During such times in our lives, we mustn't be lazy. We should try to meditate on God with one-pointedness. We should do *sahasranama archana* every day without fail, and constantly chant mantras. In this way we can greatly reduce the intensity of the suffering. Ninety percent of the difficulties we experience can be removed through our efforts.

My children, there's something else you need to remember. We should never do anything that could cause others any pain, because that will create a lot of harm. We may be hurting someone who hasn't done anything wrong. When he or she cries out with a broken heart, "Oh God, I don't know anything about this, yet they are saying these things!" that anguish will affect us in a subtle way, and will be harmful to us later. This is why it is said that we shouldn't hurt others in thought, word, or deed. Even if we cannot make others happy, we should be careful that we do not hurt anyone. This attitude will bring us divine grace.

Job opportunities are being advertised, tests held, and interviews conducted. We see the jobs being given to those who didn't do all that well in the tests or interviews. If things were happening according to our will, shouldn't those who gave the best answers get the jobs? But this doesn't always happen. So, the basis for everything is God's will. Let us therefore surrender ourselves to God's will. Those who didn't perform all that well got the jobs because the person who conducted the interview felt a certain compassion for them that he or she didn't feel for the other candidates. That compassion arose because of the candidate's previous good actions. That is God's grace. If we miss some opportunities, we shouldn't just grieve; instead we should perform good deeds, so that we can receive divine grace. We need the compassion of others, which arises from God's grace – and in order to receive this, good actions have to come from us.

We sow the seeds and add fertilizers; we dig wells and pump water in the summer for irrigation; we remove the weeds regularly. But just when the harvest time arrives, there is a flood and the entire crop is ruined. We see events like this taking place again and again. Thus, even though we make every effort, nothing comes to fruition because divine grace is absent.

Effort and grace are interrelated. We become eligible for God's grace only when we perform good actions. So, my children, allow room in your minds only for good thoughts, because our thoughts determine the nature of our actions. Let us pray to God for good thoughts to arise in us always, and for good actions to follow.

Om Namah Shivaya!

<-- *Amma praying during her birthday celebration*

Selfless service is the non-dual Truth

*The benedictory speech Amma gave in 1995 at the
inauguration of Amrita Kripa Sagar, the hospice
for terminally ill cancer patients in Mumbai.*

Salutations to all of you, who are the embodiments of love.

Seeing the hospital being inaugurated here, some of Amma's children may ask, "What is the relevance of service in the life of *sannyasa*, the life of renunciation?" My children, the truth is that compassion for the poor is our duty to God.

The sun doesn't need the light of a candle. The sun gives light to the entire world. The river doesn't have to roam around looking for water to quench its thirst. It is we who need the river's water to quench our thirst. Similarly, we need God's grace if we are to enjoy peace and harmony in life. We need to accept God's love and compassion and then to share it with others. Only in this way will our lives be filled with light.

We go to the temple to worship, and on our way out, with a hiss we drive away the destitute person who stands at the door and cries out, "Oh, I am so hungry!" My children, that is not behavior befitting devotees of God. Do not forget that being compassionate towards the needy is our duty to God.

A *sannyasi* wandered everywhere in search of God. He went to the forests, mountains, temples, and churches – but nowhere was he able to see God. In the end, he reached a deserted place and he was very tired. It was a densely wooded area and he stayed there for a few days.

And it was there that he saw a married couple walk by every day, each carrying a vessel. He saw no one else in the area. He was curious and wanted to know where they were going. So, one day he followed them secretly, and he discovered what they were doing. The couple visited a leper colony. The lepers' bodies were covered with the wounds of that terrible disease. Those people had nobody to help them and were surviving solely on the food they were occasionally given as alms. Some of them were writhing in pain. The couple went to them and lovingly talked to them. With great compassion they cleaned their wounds and gave them medicines. With their own hands, the couple fed them the food they had brought. They explained many positive things to the sick. They covered them with clean sheets. The faces of those poor, sick people lit up when they saw the couple. The love with which the couple nursed them was such that during those visits, the lepers forgot all their sorrows.

The *sannyasi* approached the couple and asked them to tell their story. They were saving a part of their salary and used that money to do this service.

For the *sannyasi*, this was the first time in his life he had experienced anything like that. Having witnessed the actions of that couple, he shouted out loud, "Today I have seen God!" and he felt so happy that he began to dance. Those who heard him were surprised: "Is he out of his mind? He says he has seen God! Where is that God? Is that leper his God?" People approached him and asked, "You say you have seen God. Who is God?" He replied, "You see, God is to be found where there is compassion. God resides in the compassionate heart. The true God is the person who has such a heart."

Amma remembers another story. There was a woman who was constantly immersed in serving those in need. But she had a doubt. She prayed, "Dear God, because of all this work, I am unable to remember You or to communicate with You even for a moment. So, do I have a place close to you?" Her eyes brimmed with tears of sadness. Suddenly she heard God's voice: "My daughter, even if it seems to you that you have no place near me, I am always close to you!"

My children, where there is selfless service God is definitely present. Some people walk around talking about *advaita* (non-duality), saying, "Isn't everything the Self? Who, then, is to love whom?" The answer to them is that *advaita* is not something to be expressed with words. *Advaita* is life. To see and love everyone as your own Self, that is true *advaita*. Then we no longer identify with our individual self – we see that we and the universe are not two, but one. This is non-duality. It is true living.

Where there is selfless action, that is where heaven is to be found. You may ask, "Isn't it enough to do selfless service? Are meditation and the repetition of a mantra necessary?" If an ordinary person is like an electric post, a *tapasvi* (a person who performs austerities) can accumulate so much strength that he or she becomes like a large transformer. By doing spiritual practice, by concentrating the mind on one point instead of thinking about unreal things, we can see our strength truly increasing. Then we don't need to search anywhere for the strength to do selfless service.

We should try to develop a mind that is like an incense stick that burns itself out while giving fragrance to the world. Only in such a mind does God spread his light. Only there will God's grace flow. We should make sure that our spiritual practice is accompanied by selfless service. That is like pouring milk into a clean vessel. On the other hand, spiritual practice without selfless service is like pouring milk into a dirty vessel. My children, don't think we can sit idly by and let others serve us.

A man saw a fox with a broken leg lying on the roadside. He felt pity for the fox and thought, "Who is going to bring food to this injured animal? Why does God do things like this so thoughtlessly?" He kept blaming God, and then he thought,

"All right, let's see if someone comes and feeds this poor animal." He moved a short distance away and sat down. A little later, a leopard appeared with a piece of meat in its mouth. It ate a part of the meat and left the remainder right next to the fox. "But will the leopard bring food again tomorrow?" the man wondered. He came again and waited there the next day. The leopard brought meat for the fox that day as well. This became a daily occurrence. The man thought, "The leopard is bringing food for the fox. From now on, I'm not going to work because someone will surely bring me food as well." He moved to another spot and sat down. A whole day went by; then another. He didn't get anything. By the third day he was very weak. He came to the point of losing his faith in God when he heard a voice say, "Son, don't be like the fox with the broken leg! Be like the leopard that brings it food!"

My children, we often think, "Let those people over there help the world," or "Let others care for the suffering." But, my dear children, to sit idly by without doing any work is an offense to God. God has given us health so that we may render service to others while remembering Him. We should develop a mind that is ready to help those who are struggling. We should always be ready to serve according to the situation. My dear children, this is the easiest way to get the vision of God. God is always within us. We don't have to roam around looking for God. But only when a discriminating intelligence awakens in us can God's will work through us. Only then can we experience even a little of His presence.

My children, until now we have worshipped the invisible God. But now God has appeared right in front of us! All around us there are people who are poor and are suffering. They are the true God! By loving them and serving them, it is God whom we love and serve!

The foremost emotion in those who come to this hospice is the fear of death. The patients who come here are those for whom all treatments have failed and who have lost all hope in life. Their souls tremble with pain and fear of death. To alleviate this, we should explain the essential truth of life to them. They need to understand that the electric current doesn't stop if the bulb breaks. Then, they will be able to take leave of this world with smiles on their faces and with peace in their hearts. Today, we are given an opportunity to do this service. Let us pray to the Almighty that everyone attains peace.

Main entrance of the AIMS hospital in Cochin, Kerala

Giving a helping hand to those who fail

Amma's benedictory speech at the inauguration of the Amrita Institute of Medical Sciences (AIMS) in Kochi, Kerala; May 1998

Salutations to all of you, who are verily the embodiments of love and the Supreme Self! Amma doesn't know any special style of speaking or advice. Yet, she will try to say something. If there are any mistakes, please forgive her.

My children, life isn't just meant for those who succeed, but also for those who fail. We see that a large section of ordinary people think and talk only about their achievements. However, for success to be lasting, we also have to think about our failures and pay attention to them.

A person who succeeds in something usually believes it is entirely due to his or her personal effort and tries to convince others of this. On the other hand, when there is failure, it is always someone else's fault. People usually say, "They didn't do what I told them to do. If they had, surely we would have succeeded!" People say this because of a wrong attitude towards failure.

When you say that someone has failed, it means that he or she has tried and has dared to take a risk. Only those who try can fail. There is risk involved in every action, for example, climbing a mountain, a baby's first steps, fishing in the ocean, studying for an examination, and learning to drive. A spirit of adventure is necessary for everything. Whatever action we undertake, success and failure will follow us like a shadow. Sometimes we succeed and sometimes we fail. Failure is not to be feared. Fear of failure will stop us from succeeding in the future; we won't able to achieve anything. This is why we must encourage those who fail. They

183

should be encouraged to try and taught not to be afraid. In sports, players are given consolation prizes even when they lose. They are given encouragement. It is always good to encourage people.

We should understand that life isn't just for winners, but also for those who lose, and we should be willing to give those who have failed a chance. We should forgive their mistakes. To be patient and forgiving is like lubricating an engine. It will help us to move forward. To dismiss those who have failed only once amounts to doing them the greatest harm. This is why it is said that not only the winners but also the losers should be given a prize in competitions. The losers shouldn't be ridiculed; they should be encouraged. To maintain enthusiasm, encouragement is essential.

Today, only winners are given a place in life. Those who fail are usually ridiculed. Amma's view is that if we wish only for success in life, that in itself is the greatest failure.

Life is for the adventurous, not for defeatists. Spirituality teaches this principle. Only if we live life according to this principle, can we create the new generation accordingly. To forgive now is to forge ahead. This elevates those who forgive as well as those who receive forgiveness.

My children, you may wonder, "Aren't we becoming like doormats? Don't we lose our sense of discrimination if we always forgive and so on?" On the contrary. It allows both sides to go forward. Only in those who understand this principle can a true attitude of selfless service be formed. True selfless service is done with a spirit of surrender. It is akin to a circle: it has no beginning or end, because it is love for the sake of love alone. With this attitude there are no expectations. In this state, we see all those who are working alongside us as gifts from God. This can happen only when love is present, and only then can we forgive others and forget their mistakes.

We know what our great ancestor Sri Rama was like. Even to his stepmother, Kaikeyi, who was responsible for his fourteen-year banishment in the forest, his response was to prostrate before her and ask for her blessings before he departed. Lord Krishna gave liberation to the hunter whose arrow became instrumental in his leaving his body. The Lord forgave the man for his ignorance. That is what Jesus Christ was like as well. He knew Judas would betray him, yet he didn't hesitate to wash the feet of Judas and kiss them.

These are the examples shown by our ancestors. If we use them as models, we can certainly experience peace in our lives.

The path for the progress of the nation

Many people ask the question, "How can I dedicate myself to the benefit of the world and for the progress of our nation?" This country will develop and grow only if we can create strong, energetic, and dedicated individuals. In fact, this is what Krishna did. He gave Arjuna, the great archer-warrior, the strength, vitality, and efficiency to fight unrighteousness, untruth and deceit. He transformed Arjuna's very attitude towards life. Because he was ready to follow the Lord's words, Arjuna didn't have to blame the circumstances he faced; nor did he flee from them. Instead, he fought untiringly and moved forward.

Lord Buddha achieved this too. He created many buddhas. Christ did the same thing. Those great souls created benefactors for the world when they were on earth, and they continue to do so even though they have left this world.

The greatest gift we can offer the nation is the creation of such a future generation. The growth or decay of the nation depends on the strength of the coming generation.

Throughout life, we should have the attitude of being a beginner. Nowadays, our bodies have grown, but our minds have not. For the mind to grow as large as the universe, we have to maintain

185

the inner attitude of a child. Only a child can develop, because of his or her innocence. It is this innocence and absence of ego that we should nurture. Only then can we become recipients of God's grace.

The basis for everything is the Universal Power, which juggles with us, and sometimes raises us to great heights. We then gain name and fame. But if that Universal Power doesn't support us, we will fall down and be smashed. We should always be aware of this. Amma remembers a story in this context.

Some pebbles lay in a pile by the road. A child passed by, picked up one of the pebbles, and threw it up in the air. As it was going up, the pebble began to feel proud. "Look at me! All the other pebbles are lying down there. I'm the only one flying like this high in the sky, moving with the sun and the moon!" The pebble started mocking the pebbles on the ground. "Why are you still lying there? Come on up!" The other pebbles consoled themselves, "What can we do? He was lying here with us just a moment ago. Now look at his status! Well, you need luck for everything!" But the high-flying pebble couldn't continue boasting for long. As the power of the throw ceased, the pebble started falling. As it fell to the ground, it said to the others, "You see! I felt bad about being away from you all. That's why I came back and didn't stay up there for long!" Always finding a justification for everything, the tendency to justify even a fall, never admitting one's mistakes – this is what we see in today's world.

There is wisdom within us, but we are seldom able to put it into practice. When a doctor made a house visit, he was offered a Coca-Cola and coconut water to drink. He chose the Coca-Cola and not the fresh coconut water. He knew that coconut water is the best thing for thirst and that Coca-Cola is bad for the body. But Coca-Cola has become fashionable, so he ignored the coconut water. Likewise, even though we have knowledge, it is not reflected in our actions. We have to turn our knowledge into action, because only then will it be of any benefit.

Today, everyone knows only how to take. The willingness to give is absent in most people. A man fell into a pit. "Save me! Save me!" he cried. A passerby heard him and came to the rescue. In order to lift the man out of the pit, he said, "Give me your hand!" But the man in the pit wouldn't give him his hand. Finally the rescuer extended his own hand and said, "Take hold of my hand!" Immediately the man grabbed hold of his hand. This is what most of us are like. We are only willing to take, and are very reluctant when it comes to giving. If this attitude persists, it will lead to the downfall of the country. Perhaps we can't inspire others only to give instead of taking, but we can at least try to inspire them to give something. This is the way to maintain the harmony in this country and in the world at large. My children, you need to understand this and persevere. Only then can the country progress.

With His hands and feet everywhere

God isn't someone sitting on a ceremonial throne somewhere up beyond the sky. God is beyond the intellect. God is an *experience*. We cannot see God with our eyes, but if we are inwardly attentive, we can see Him. God's presence can be seen in the singing cuckoo, the cawing crow, the rumbling ocean, and the roaring lion. The same Supreme Consciousness lies behind the walking feet, the working hands, the speaking tongue, the seeing eyes, and the beating heart. The Supreme Consciousness fills everything everywhere. This reminds Amma of a story.

In a certain village stood a statue of a saint. The arms of the statue were stretched out, and at the foot of the statue were written these words: *Come into my arms!* After many years, the statue lost both arms. This troubled the villagers. But *Come into my arms!* could still clearly be read. Some of the villagers suggested, "Let us erect a new statue." Others disagreed and said, "No, let us restore the old statue and give it new arms." An old man came forward and said, "Don't get into a fight over this. There's no need for new arms or a new statue." The others asked, "In that case, what would be the meaning of the words that are written on the statue, *Come into my arms!*" The old man replied, "That's no problem. Just add a few words below those words, saying, *I have no other arms than yours. My arms work through yours.*"

Likewise, God has no hands or feet of His own. God acts through us. So, we have to bring God into our hands and feet. And we need to bring God into our heart and tongue.

We ourselves have to become God

Two things normally happen in life – we perform actions and we experience the fruits of those actions. While good actions bring good results, negative actions will certainly bring bad results. Do not be scared by these words, my children. If we take one step towards God, He will take ten steps towards us.

In village schools, the students are often given grace marks in the examinations to help them pass. Those who have written at least some of the answers can get a passing grade in this way. Similarly, there has to be some effort on our part. If that effort has been made, success is sure to follow because God's grace will flow to us. More than our effort, God's grace is the reason for our success. God's grace is what adds the sweetness to our effort.

Along with our effort, we should also try to eliminate the 'I' in us. Only then can we receive God's grace. Even if God showers His grace on us, it will be a waste if the sense of 'I' remains in us. People apply for jobs, and those who pass the test are called for an interview. Many applicants who satisfy the height and weight requirements appear for the interview with their academic certificates and excellent references. But those who answer the questions faultlessly are not always selected for the job. The reason is that some of them didn't elicit the grace that softens the heart of the interviewer. That grace is acquired as the fruit of good actions. There are many who try the easy way out to get what they want, without trying to win that grace.

It is said that ten million earthly rupees equals one heavenly paisa. And one second of heavenly time is equal to ten million years on earth. A devotee prayed to God, "God, are You not the abode of compassion? You don't have to give me much. Just bless me by giving me one paisa from Your world!" God replied, "Of course, I am happy to give you a paisa. Just wait a second!"

This is what happens when we try to fool God. But God is no fool! God is the great Intelligence that is the source of all intelligence in the universe. We should remember this. So, the easy way to achieve success in life is to become eligible for God's grace by performing good actions.

While doing any action, we should obey the voice of our conscience. Whatever we do against our conscience, ignoring that voice, will lead to turmoil within us. It will only lead to our ruin.

Humility and compassion

Amma always says that meditation is as valuable as gold. Meditation leads to material prosperity, peace, and liberation. Even a moment spent in meditation is never a waste – it can only be of great value. If, in addition to our meditation, we also have compassion, it is like gold with a fragrance! A smiling face, a kind word, a compassionate glance – all this is truly meditation. Even a casual word from us carries great importance! So, each word of ours should be uttered with great care. We should be careful not to utter even one word that could cause another person pain, because whatever we give comes back to us. If we give sorrow to others, we will be given sorrow. If we give love, joy and love will be ours.

A group of travelers once lost their way and found themselves in an unfamiliar place. They met a man on the road and asked the way. Rudely they said, "Hey, you! How do we get to that place?" Hearing their arrogant tone, the man decided to give those haughty fellows the run around, and he directed them to go round in a circle.

Had they curbed their arrogance and asked politely, the man would have tried to help. He would have taken them to someone who knew the way even if he himself didn't know. So, the response we get from others is determined by our attitude towards them and the words we use. If we speak with love and humility, we get a suitable response. This is why it is said that every word we use should be chosen with great care.

A man goes to a certain neighborhood looking for a job. "I am a poor man. I am unemployed. Please give me some work!" he begs. But the people drive him away. The poor man goes to another locality. But the people there shout at him and order him to leave. If this experience is repeated ten times, the man may not even want to live anymore. He will want to commit suicide. But suppose someone lovingly says to him, "Be patient. If anything comes up, I will definitely call you!" This may save his life. We should therefore make sure that every thought and word of ours is filled with love and compassion. God's grace automatically flows into such people. "O God, let no one be harmed by my thoughts, glances, or words!" Such heartfelt prayer is what true devotion is all about. This is true knowledge, our real duty to God.

The sun doesn't need the light of a candle. God doesn't need anything from us. All that God expects from us is a compassionate heart. We should go out amongst those who suffer and bring them peace. This is what God wants. It is our loving kindness towards those who suffer that makes us eligible for the grace of the Supreme Spirit.

Amma doesn't want to disturb you by talking any longer. Amma cannot claim that all the institutions of this ashram have come into being because of Amma's ability. We are able to do all these things because of the abilities of the devotees, children like you. Thousands of Amma's children toil for eighteen hours a day without a salary. Not even this hospital was built by contracting it out to someone. Amma's children worked according to their abilities. Some mistakes were made at first, but no one was removed for that reason. Because of that encouragement, and by God's grace, they were able to correct the errors and complete the job beautifully. Let us give those who fail another chance and uplift them instead of rejecting them. By giving those who have failed a hand, we can raise them to the ranks of winners.

Shiva…Shiva… Shiva.

Make every day an Onam festival

Amma's Onam message 1998 Amritapuri

Today, it is Onam, a day of festivity, excitement, enthusiasm, and joy. It is a day during which even the most miserable people try to forget their suffering. It is said that to remember by forgetting is real remembrance. If a doctor keeps remembering his wife and children while doing surgery, the surgery will not succeed. If the operation is to succeed, he has to focus totally on the work he is doing. Likewise, when he comes home and his child comes running to him for his love, calling out "Daddy! Daddy!" – if his mind is then still focused on his patients, he can't be a good father. And if he doesn't listen to his wife when she tells him about her problems, he cannot be a good husband either. The doctor forgets his home while at the hospital, and forgets the hospital while at home. It is with his ability to forget that he achieves success at work and happiness in life.

Is it enough that we rejoice only on the holy day of Onam? Shouldn't life be joyful every day? To be happy for just one day a year and sad on all other days – is happiness possible only for one day? Are we then really happy even on that one day? Think about this, my children!

Not just one day, but all three hundred and sixty five days of the year should be filled with joy. Our entire lives should become a festival! Spirituality teaches us the way to accomplish this. For this surrender to take place, total refuge in the Supreme Being is required. This is what Mahabali really showed us. He was an *asura*, but he was able to surrender himself – his sense of 'I' – to the Supreme Being. God doesn't ask anything other than that from us.

God is the personification of compassion, standing humbly with both arms extended towards us to receive our ego. The ego is what God likes the most as an offering from us, and that is what we should offer to God. This is what Mahabali did. If we are not ready to do this, then God will somehow extract the ego from us! God knows that only when this is done can we experience true happiness. This surrender to the Supreme Spirit brings about the purification of the mind and intellect. This is how we can transform life into a festival.

It is said that only when there is sacrifice in life is it possible to be happy. There are many small sacrifices in life. Cricket fans are ready to withstand rain and scorching sun to see a match. When a baby is sick, the parents stay up all night and nurse the child, even if they have worked all day and are exhausted. These are the little sacrifices we make. But, to attain supreme joy, which lasts forever, a great sacrifice – the sacrifice of the ego – is necessary.

Only through sacrifice will we find happiness. From a small sacrifice we experience a joy that lasts for a short while; it is not everlasting. You may remember the story that many of you were told as children. It is the story of the clod of clay and the dry leaf who were playing hide and seek. It is a story for small children, but it has a great meaning. As the clod and the leaf were playing, a wind began to blow. The clod got very worried and thought, "Oh, no! The leaf could get blown away!" The clod sat on top of the leaf and saved it. A little later, it suddenly began to rain. The leaf sat on top of the clod and sheltered it from the rain, and the clod was saved. But then the wind and the rain came together and you know what happened. The leaf was blown away and the clod dissolved in the rain. This is what our lives are like. When we depend on others, we are given small measures of happiness, but if we are faced with a great danger, there won't be anyone there to save us. Then, our only recourse will be to take refuge in the Supreme Being. That surrender is our sole protection. It is the only way to maintain happiness throughout life.

Live in this moment

My children, we may carry many burdens of sorrow – the son hasn't found a job, the daughter isn't married, we haven't built the house we dreamed of, we don't get cured of our illness, there is family discord, the business is running at a loss, and so on. We burn like rice husks, thinking about all our troubles.[47] The mind is tense, and this tension is the cause of all diseases. The only way to remove this tension is to surrender. What is the use of undergoing all that stress and suffering? We need to perform our actions to the best of our ability, using the strength that God has given us, and then let things unfold according to God's will. Leave everything to the Supreme Being. Taking total refuge in God is the only way. There's no use in letting yourself burn, thinking about what is gone and what is yet to come. Only this present moment is with you. Be careful not to lose this moment because of your sorrow.

'Tomorrow' will never come. Only *this moment* is our own to experience. We don't even know if we will be able to take another breath. My dear children, we should try to live in the present moment.

This doesn't mean that we don't have to plan for the future. Before building a house, we have to make a plan. While drawing the plan, our full attention should be on it, and when we build the house, our attention should be on that. This is what Amma means.

We have to draw a plan for the bridge before we build it. At that point we don't spend time focusing our attention on the construction; we focus on the plan. And later when we build the

---

[47] Rice husks burn for a long time.

bridge, our full attention is on that. Getting ready for the future is certainly good, but what is the use of getting over-anxious about what is yet to come? The important thing is that we spend this moment usefully and happily. Amma is talking about the way to do this. We have to live this moment that we have now in a manner that will give the utmost joy to the world and to ourselves.

In order to experience joy at this moment, we have to forget what is past and what is yet to come. This is possible if we have total surrender to the Supreme Being. Then life will become a festival. It will be Onam three hundred and sixty-five days a year!

So, my children, let us offer ourselves to the Supreme Being, and make life itself a festival.

Refining the mind

My children, even though we take pride in being human, that applies only to the external form. Within we are still the great ape! Our minds are still the minds of monkeys! When the human fetus is in the womb, it is first formed like a fish and then like a monkey – and, then, having been born as a human, we are reluctant to give up our monkey nature.

A monkey in a tree leaps from one branch to another. But the human monkey is far superior to this, for in one leap he reaches the moon. With another leap he lands in America, and with the next in Russia. He leaps many years into the past, and then the next moment jumps into the future. This is how the monkey of the human mind behaves! To transform such a mind is no small task. The power of our prior *samskara* is that great.

Three men were walking along a road. Their names were Ramu, Damu, and Komu. As they walked, someone called from behind, "Hey, Ramu!" Ramu looked back. After some distance, someone else called out, "Hey, Damu!" This time Damu looked back. After a while they heard, "Hey, Komu!" and Komu looked back. As they continued on, someone suddenly called, "Hey, you monkeys!" It is said that all three of them looked back!

This is a prior innate tendency. The human being has a monkey mind, a mind that constantly runs in different directions – and it is very difficult to change. To be able to control such a mind, it has to be bent into a circle – i.e., the thoughts that are running far and wide have to be put in order and they have to be controlled – and the qualities that are needed to achieve this are humbleness and surrender. If we have these qualities, our thoughts will not wander as they please. If a snake puts its tail in its mouth, it cannot move forward. Likewise, if we can bend our minds to our will, unwanted thoughts will disappear and our minds will be under our control.

Mahabali had the humility to bow his head in front of the Supreme Spirit. He was able to surrender to God. As a result, his mind became as expansive as the universe, and love and compassion filled his being. Thus he evolved from the demonic state to the state of divinity.

We, too, can evolve from our present monkey mind to the level of God. All we need to do is surrender to God. We have to be willing to bow our heads before God. We have to develop humility. Amma so often tells you that our bodies have grown, but not our minds. This is our present state. For the mind to become as expansive as the universe, we first have to become like children, because only a child can grow.

When we connect a pipe to a tank, all the water in the tank flows out – and the water that was in the tank benefits the world. Similarly, we have to become connected to the Supreme Spirit. Then God's infinite power will flow through us. To connect to the Supreme Spirit is to discard the sense of 'I' and to surrender everything to God. With the attitude that we are nothing, we truly become everything. This is the meaning of saying "If you are a zero, you become a hero."

A devotee must have the following qualities: he or she should be humble toward others, feel a sense of reverence towards all living beings, have compassion, and always have the attitude of being a beginner. This is the culture that the ancient *Rishis* bestowed on us. If we imbibe these qualities and live accordingly, we can reach the ultimate goal of life.

Glossary

Advaita – Non-dualism. The philosophy which teaches that the Creator and creation are one and indivisible.

Archana – 'Offering for worship. 'A form of worship in which the names of a deity are chanted, usually 108, 300 or 1000 names in one sitting.

Arjuna – The third of the five Pandava brothers. A great archer who is one of the heroes of the Mahabharata. He was Krishna's friend and disciple. It is Arjuna whom Krishna is addressing in the Bhagavad Gita.

Ashram – 'Place of striving.' A place where spiritual aspirants live or visit in order to lead a spiritual life and engage in spiritual practice. It is usually the home of a spiritual master, saint, or ascetic, who guides the aspirants.

Asura – A demon; a person with demonic qualities.

Atman – The transcendental Self, Spirit, or Consciousness, which is eternal; our essential nature. One of the fundamental tenets of Sanatana Dharma is that we are the eternal, pure, unblemishable Self (Spirit).

Avatar – 'Descent.' An incarnation of the Supreme Being. The aim of a God-incarnation is to protect the good, destroy evil, restore righteousness in the world, and lead humanity to the spiritual goal of Self-realization. It is very rare for an incarnation to be a full descent (*Purnavatar*).

Bhagavad Gita – 'Song of the Lord.' Bhagavad = of the Lord; gita = song; referring particularly to advice. The teachings that Krishna gave Arjuna on the Kurukshetra battlefield at the beginning of the Mahabharata war. It is a practical guide for the daily life of everyone, and contains the essence of Vedic wisdom. Commonly referred to as the Gita.

Bhagavatam – One of eighteen scriptures known as the Puranas, dealing especially with the incarnations of Vishnu, and, in great detail, with the life of Sri Krishna. It emphasizes the path of devotion. Also known as the Srimad Bhagavatam.

Bhakti – Devotion.

Bhava – Divine mood, attitude, or state.

Bhima – The second oldest of the five Pandava brothers, whose story is described in the Mahabharata.

Brahmachari – A celibate disciple who practices spiritual disciplines and is usually being trained by a Guru.

Brahman – The Absolute Reality; the Whole; Supreme Being; 'That' which encompasses and pervades everything, which is One and indivisible.

Darshan – An audience with or a vision of the Divine or a holy person.

Dhanvantari – He appears in the Vedas and Puranas as the physician of the celestial beings (*devas*), and is the deity of medicine.

Dharma – From the root *dhri*; to support, uphold, hold onto. Often translated simply as 'righteousness.' *Dharma* has many profoundly interrelated meanings: that which upholds the universe, the laws of Truth, the universal laws, the laws of nature, in accordance with divine harmony, righteousness, religion, duty, responsibility, right conduct, justice, goodness, and truth. *Dharma* signifies the inner principles of religion. It signifies the true nature, proper functions and actions of a being or object. It is, for example, the *dharma* of fire to burn. The *dharma* of a human being is to live in harmony with the universal spiritual principles and to cultivate a higher consciousness.

Gopi – The *gopis* were cowherd girls and milkmaids who lived in Vrindavan. They were Krishna's closest devotees and were known for their supreme devotion to the Lord. They exemplify the most intense love for God.

Grihasthashrami – A person who is dedicated to a spiritual life while living the life of a householder.

Ishta Devata – 'Beloved Deity.' The Divinity one has chosen to worship in accordance with one's own nature, and which is the object of one's greatest desire and ultimate goal.

Ithihasa – 'So it was.' Epic history, particularly the Ramayana and Mahabharata. This term sometimes refers to the Puranas, especially the Skanda Purana and the Srimad Bhagavatam.

Kali Yuga – 'Age of Darkness.' There is a cycle of four ages or time periods in creation (see *Yuga* in glossary). We are presently living in the *Kali Yuga*. Human civilization degenerates spiritually and unrighteousness prevails throughout the *Kali Yuga*. It is referred to as the Dark Age, mainly because people are the furthest possible from God.

Krishna – 'He who draws us to himself'; 'the Dark One.' ('Dark' in this context refers to his boundlessness, and the fact that he is unknowable and incomprehensible to the very limited range of the mind and intellect.) He was born into a royal family, but grew up with foster parents and lived as a young cowherd in Vrindavan, where he was loved and worshipped by his devoted companions, the *gopis* (milkmaids and cowherd girls) and *gopas* (cowherd boys). Krishna later became the ruler of Dwaraka. He was a friend of and adviser to his cousins, the Pandavas, and especially Arjuna, to whom he revealed his teachings in the Bhagavad Gita.

Kuchela – Kuchela was a childhood friend of Lord Krishna. As an adult, Kuchela lived in poverty. His wife and children were starving. One day Kuchela's wife said to him, "Was not Lord Krishna your classmate? Go to him and ask for help." Kuchela agreed. But how could he go empty-handed to see his old friend? There was nothing in his house to give except a handful of flat, beaten rice. Kuchela left for Mathura with the beaten rice as his only gift. On his way, he wondered how Krishna would receive him. Krishna was famous and lived in a palace while he, Kuchela, lived in utter poverty. But as soon as Krishna saw Kuchela, he ran forward and embraced him. He invited Kuchela inside the palace and treated him with great affection. Kuchela was hesitant to offer the handful of beaten rice. But Krishna grabbed it, ate it, and offered it to others, and he praised the taste. Kuchela spent four days happily in the palace. He completely forgot to ask Krishna to relieve his poverty. But when he reached home he discovered that Krishna had sent gold and rich clothes and money to his house, and a splendid mansion was built for Kuchela.

Mahabali – Mahabali is celebrated on the festival day of Onam. Mahabali was a powerful *asura* king who defeated the *devas* in battle and extended his dominion over the celestial realm. Aditi, the mother of all *devas*, was worried about the fate of her progeny and prayed to Lord Vishnu to save them. Lord Vishnu took birth as her son in the form of Vamana, the Divine Dwarf-Boy. Vamana, as a *brahmachari*, visited Mahabali, who welcomed him and promised him any gift he wanted. Vamana asked only for as much land as he could cover with three footsteps. Mahabali considered this to be a trivial request, but granted Vamana the land, despite his Guru's warning that the young *brahmachari* was none other than the Lord Himself who had come in disguise. As Vamana began to measure the land with his steps, he grew to an immense size and covered all the worlds in just two paces. As there was no space for the third step, Mahabali gladly surrendered to the Lord and offered his head as a possible place for the Lord to place His foot. In the popular version of the story, the Lord pushed Mahabali down to the netherworld with His foot. But as Amma points out, this is not the correct interpretation of the story, and it doesn't happen this way in the Srimad Bhagavatam. The Lord's real motive was to destroy the ego of Mahabali who, in all other respects, was a great devotee of His. In the Bhagavatam, Mahabali is given a very special place in the world of Sutala, to which he retreats along with his distinguished grandfather, Prahlada, one of the Lord's greatest devotees. The Lord Himself promises to stay as Mahabali's doorkeeper in that splendid world. The essence of the story is that the Lord blesses His devotee by destroying the devotee's ego, and elevates him or her to the supreme state. It is said that Mahabali requested to the Lord that he be allowed to visit his dear subjects once a year, and Onam is the day on which he makes that visit. According to the legend, Mahabali was a great ruler under whom everyone was equal and prosperous, and on Onam day, the people of Kerala remember his golden rule. This association of Mahabali's name with a special festival happens only in Kerala. The Bhagavatam makes no mention of a request by Mahabali to visit his subjects annually.

Mahatma – 'Great soul.' When Amma uses the word *mahatma,* she is referring to a Self-realized soul.

Onam – Onam is the most important festival in Kerala. It is celebrated in the first month of the Malayalam calendar year and has the character of the New Year and harvest festival celebrations. Everyone, regardless of caste or creed or wealth, rejoices and celebrates on this day, wearing new clothes and enjoying special meals. Onam marks the annual return of the spirit of the mythical King Mahabali to his kingdom.

Pada puja – The worship of God's, the Guru's or a saint's feet. As the feet support the body, the Guru Principle supports the Supreme Truth. The Guru's feet thus represent the Supreme Truth.

Payasam – A sweet rice pudding.

Prarabdha – 'Responsibilities, burdens.' The fruit of past actions from this and past lives that will manifest in this life.

Puja – 'Adoration.' Sacred ritual; ceremonial worship.

Radha – One of Krishna's *gopis.* She was closer to Krishna than any other *gopi* and personifies the highest and purest love for God.

Rahu – One of the *navagrahas* (nine planets). Rahu is the ascending lunar node. In Hindu mythology, Rahu is a serpent that swallows the sun or the moon, causing eclipses.

Rama – 'Giver of Joy.' The divine hero in the epic Ramayana. He was an incarnation of Lord Vishnu, and is considered to be the ideal of *dharma* and virtue.

Ramayana – 'The life of Rama.' One of India's two great Indian historical epics (the other being the Mahabharata), depicting the life of Rama, written by Valmiki. Rama was an incarnation of Vishnu. A major part of the epic describes how Sita, Rama's wife, was abducted and taken to Sri Lanka by Ravana, the demon king, and how she was rescued by Rama and his devotees, including his great devotee Hanuman.

Rishi – *Rsi* = to know. Self-realized seer. Usually refers to the seven *Rishis* of ancient India, i.e., Self-realized souls who could 'see' the Supreme Truth.

Sabarimala – A pilgrimage center in Kerala with a famous temple dedicated to Lord Ayyappan.

Samadhi – A state of deep, one-pointed concentration, in which all thoughts subside and the mind enters into a state of complete stillness in which only Pure Consciousness remains, as one abides in the *Atman* (Self). It is described as a state in which the experiencer, the experience, and that which is experienced are one.

Samsara – The ongoing cycle of birth, death, and rebirth.

Samskara – *Samskara* has two meanings: the totality of impressions imprinted on the mind by experiences from this or previous lives, which influence the life of a human being – his or her nature, actions, state of mind, etc.; the kindling of the right understanding (knowledge) within each person, leading to the refinement of his or her character.

Sanatana Dharma – The Eternal Religion; the Eternal Principle. The traditional name for Hinduism.

Sankalpa – A creative, integral resolve which is manifested. The sankalpa of an ordinary person does not always yield the corresponding fruit, but a *sankalpa* made by a Self-realized being inevitably manifests its aimed result.

Sannyasi or **sannyasini** – A monk or nun who has taken formal vows of renunciation; traditionally wears ochre-colored clothes, representing the burning away of all attachments.

Satsang – *Sat* = truth, being; *sanga* = association with. Being in the company of the holy, wise, and virtuous. Also a spiritual discourse by a sage or scholar.

Seva – Selfless service.

Sita – The wife of Rama. She is considered a perfect model of virtue for women.

Sri Lalita Sahasranama: A sacred text consisting of the 1000 names of the Divine Mother, which is chanted. Each name is a mantra.

Tapas – 'Heat.' Self-discipline, austerities, penance, and self sacrifice; spiritual practices which burn up the impurities of the mind.

Tapasvi – A serious practitioner of *tapas.*

Vanaprastha – The reclusive stage of life. In the ancient Indian tradition, there are four stages of life. First the youngster is sent to a *gurukula*, where he or she lives the life of a *brahmachari*. Then he or she gets married and lives as a householder, dedicated to spiritual life (*grihasthashrami*). *Vanaprastha* is the third stage of life. When the couple's children are old enough to take care of themselves, the parents retreat to a hermitage or an ashram, where they live a purely spiritual life, doing spiritual practice. During the fourth stage of life, they renounce the world completely and live the life of *sannyasis*.

Vedanga – Branches of knowledge that are auxiliary to the Vedas.

Vedanta – 'Veda conclusion.' The philosophy of the Upanishads, the concluding part of the Vedas, which holds the Ultimate Truth to be 'One without a second.'

Vedantin – A person who follows the path of Vedanta.

Vedas – 'Knowledge, wisdom.' The ancient, sacred scriptures of Hinduism. A collection of holy texts in Sanskrit, which are divided into four parts: Rig, Yajur, Sama and Atharva. The Vedas, which are among the world's oldest scriptures, consist of 100,000 verses, as well as additional prose. They were brought into the world by the *Rishis,* who were Self-realized sages. The Vedas are considered to be the direct revelation of the Supreme Truth.

Viveka – Discrimination; the ability to discriminate between the real and the unreal, between the eternal and the transient, *dharma* and *adharma* (unrighteousness), etc.

Yudhisthira – The oldest of the five Pandava brothers. He was king of Hastinapura and Indraprastha. He was known for his unblemished piety.

Yuga – Age or eon. There are four *yugas*: the *Satya* or *Krita Yuga* (the Golden Age), *Treta Yuga, Dwapara Yuga,* and *Kali Yuga* (the Dark Age). We are presently living in the *Kali Yuga.* The *yugas* are said to succeed each other almost endlessly.